The pound ar

Manchester University Press

The *Manchester Capitalism* book series

Manchester Capitalism is a series of books which follows the trail of money and power across the systems of our failing capitalism. The books make powerful interventions about who gets what and why in a research-based and solidly argued way that is accessible for the concerned citizen. They go beyond critique of neo liberalism and its satellite knowledges to re-frame our problems and offer solutions about what is to be done.

Manchester was the city of Engels and Free Trade where the twin philosophies of collectivism and free market liberalism were elaborated. It is now the home of this venture in radical thinking that challenges self-serving elites. We see the provincial radicalism rooted here as the ideal place from which to cast a cold light on the big issues of economic renewal, financial reform and political mobilisation.

General editors: Julie Froud and Karel Williams

Already published:

The end of the experiment: From competition to the foundational economy

What a waste: Outsourcing and how it goes wrong

Licensed larceny: Infrastructure, financial extraction and the global South

The econocracy: The perils of leaving economics to the experts

Reckless opportunists: Elites at the end of the establishment

Foundational economy: The infrastructure of everyday life

Safe as houses: Private greed, political negligence and housing policy after Grenfell

The spatial contract: A new politics of provision for an urbanized planet

The pound and the fury

Why anger and confusion reign in an economy paralysed by myth

Jack Mosse

Manchester University Press

Published by Manchester University Press
Altrincham Street, Manchester M1 7JA

www.manchesteruniversitypress.co.uk

British Library Cataloguing-in-Publication Data
A catalogue record for this book is available from the British Library

ISBN 978 1 5261 5880 2 paperback

First published 2021

Typeset
by New Best-set Typesetters Ltd
Printed in Great Britain
by TJ Books Ltd, Padstow

'Sound and fury (signifying nothing).' Much furious talk, of no importance or little or no meaning. (E. Partridge, *A Dictionary of Clichés*, Routledge, 1940)

It is a tale
Told by an idiot, full of sound and fury,
Signifying nothing.
(*Macbeth*, v, v, 26–28)

For Monica

Contents

Figures

Acknowledgements

Special thanks to: Aeron Davis, Karel Williams, Thomas Dark, Julie Froud, Anna Killick, Liz Moor, John Clark, Oliver James, Simon Hopper, Ben Harvey, Jacob Rollinson, Jo Littler, Mike Berry, Jo Cook and Mark Lamont.

Acknowledgements

Introduction

In my lifetime I have witnessed something of a revolution in how we think about language. There is, now more than ever, an appreciation and awareness of the power of language. There is evidence of this collective enlightenment everywhere: many of us are now given training in how to use the correct sort of language at work; people worry about using the most up-to-date terms; everyone seems to have an opinion about something controversial a public figure said (Was it or wasn't it ok? Is the outrage justified? What's the significance of their words?). Both in the media and in everyday conversations, statements that would have been common place 30–40 years ago are now condemned and can rightly cause those making them to lose their jobs, or to be dropped from a social circle. Language has taken on a significance it didn't previously have; it is recognised as something that shapes our world, and as something that can be as harmful as a physical weapon.

Going further back, we can see that hand in hand with this recognition of the power of language has been a movement towards exposing the absurdity of the assumptions that prop up racist, sexist or homophobic world views. Concepts that had previously been regarded as unquestioned facts were, and are, being deconstructed and exposed as resting upon nothing more solid than fable. Once we see that there is no reason behind the discrimination – no reason to think that women are less intelligent than men, that Africans are genetically inferior to Europeans, that homosexuality is 'un-natural' – we see that there is no reason for discrimination based on gender, race or sexuality. It is through understanding the power of language, and dispelling the myths that support these absurd and vicious assumptions, that we can move beyond them.

Yet, whilst the *culture wars* have led to, and continue to push for, greater equality in regards to race, gender and sexual orientation, there is one area of society that has been left untouched by this march towards a fairer world. And that is the area, which – as one of the people I spoke to for this book put it – 'decides what goes where and who gets what'. The economy, and the myths that prop it up, have been ignored by the movement to expose and deconstruct the myths that generate discrimination and inequality in other areas of our society. Laws have been passed to try to ensure equality in these 'cultural' realms, while at the same time other laws have been passed and polices pursued to ensure inequality in the sphere of 'what goes where and who gets what'.

The reason the economy has been hermeneutically sealed off from this push towards equality is because the economy is seen as a fundamentally separate category from the culture war issues. It is presented as a different ball game altogether. Economic inequality, unlike race, gender or sexuality, is not seen to be something that language has much involvement in. However, this is wrong, and myth, just as it backs up other aspects of discrimination, backs up our deeply unequal and discriminative economy.

JFK knew it. And Roland Barthes knew it. And they knew how myth derives its power. They understood that it works by hiding the everyday assumptions that underlie our world views. That it draws a line over the fragility of the truths that those assumptions are constructed upon, and gives them the solidity to act as foundations for other equally frail assumptions. That myth encapsulates one view of the world and gives it the presence to form the unquestioned basis of other views and behaviours. Unquestioned myth: Africans are genetically inferior to Europeans. Behaviours and views that stem from this unquestioned myth: colonialism, slavery, racism.

One of Barthes' classic examples is taken from the front page of a 1955 copy of *Paris-Match*. On the cover a young black boy in French military uniform proudly salutes what we assume to be an out of frame tricolour. The image freezes and solidifies a controversial vision of the world – a myth that the colonies are grateful towards the colonisers. Yet, unless you take the time to deconstruct and break the image down, you wouldn't see how this works, how the image sweeps away the complex, violent and oppressive history of the French empire, and naturalises a distorted notion of colonialism. You would just see a black boy in French uniform saluting the tricolour, and this would reinforce the myth of the benevolent empire and act as a justification for its continued presence.

It is in this way, through mundane repetition, that myths cover up alternative histories and become dominant frameworks for understanding the world. Through this mundane and unseen repetition, hidden assumptions behind our belief structures are formed and solidified – assumptions that frequently mask the historical precedent of power relations and discrimination.

Consider JFK as he addresses the graduating students at Yale a few years after the publication of Barthes' celebrated mythological analysis:

> As every past generation has had to disenthrall itself from an inheritance of truisms and stereotypes, so in our own time we must move on from the reassuring repetition of stale phrases to a new, difficult, but essential confrontation with reality. For the great enemy of the truth is very often not the lie – deliberate, contrived, and dishonest – but the myth – persistent, persuasive, and unrealistic. Too often we hold fast to the clichés of our forebears. We subject all facts to a prefabricated set of interpretations. We enjoy the comfort of opinion without the discomfort of thought.[1]

We bring, as I will argue in this book, a 'prefabricated set of interpretations' to how we think about the economy. Interpretations that are based on nothing more than myth, and interpretations that mask the discriminative and unequal set of power relations behind how our economy functions.

It is possible to make this argument, because, while knowledge of the economy is not based on solid incontrovertible scientific truth, there is enough there to observe, even to a non-economist like myself, that some things are based on myth, and some things are not. This book therefore addresses the problem of myth in two ways: it explores it from an anthropological perspective by looking at how we understand our economy. It then exposes the myth behind our understanding, by outlining some fundamentals about how the economy actually works.

The first four chapters are based on the many conversations I had with various people from different sections of society about the economy. These included (among many others): traders, treasury officials, bank directors, financial journalists, caretakers, youth workers and florists. In talking to such a broad range of people I began to see the economy as something that means different things to different people. For instance, Aaron, a financial journalist, understands the economy as:

> this beast that we are incapable of understanding ... it functions as this thing that is apart from us, it's not meant to be centrally controlled: it's this amorphous thing that keeps evolving.

Whilst Tracy, a single mother living on a housing estate in north London, described the economy like this:

> Rich wealthy men decide what goes where, what we get, what we don't get, what gets spent, where it gets spent and how it gets spent.

And for Thomas, an economist working in the civil service, the economy is:

> the process and mechanisms that we use to redistribute and incentivise.

Despite these differences, I argue that it is possible to trace an overarching myth that lies behind the disparate economic visions I found. This myth, as I will show, is the idea of the economy as something akin to a pot of money or household budget – as an existential factor that exercises discipline over how we live.

The need to explore and expose this myth has become increasingly prescient. At the time of writing, the COVID-19 crisis is necessitating a scale of government intervention in the economy not seen since the Second World War. It is unclear how the government will seek to pay for this intervention and service its debts or deal with the recession caused by shutting down vast sections of the private sector. Will we be plunged into more years of austerity? Or will they choose a different way out? The path taken will determine how we live for decades to come.

Even edging back from the urgency of rebuilding after COVID-19, it's possible to see that the crisis only amplifies an already critical situation. As we seek to start life outside the EU and face up to the climate crisis, there are a number of economic choices about how we want to live that need to be taken sooner rather than later. Even without COVID-19, we would be at a generation-defining crossroads.

Yet, as argued in the following pages, myth pollutes our understanding of the economy, keeping us in the dark and unable to assess the economic choices that stand before us. If we are to move into the light, and see through the myth, change must come in the form of our most powerful institutions adopting a clearer and more honest approach towards economic communication.

Chapter 1 starts with the most obvious example of the myth by drawing on the conversations I had with the 'everyday' people on the council estate next to where I was living. This is where the anger and confusion in the book's subtitle derive their meaning, as the people I spoke to on the estate were furious, and confused, about how the economy works. Through these conversations and other research that looks at 'everyday' understandings of the economy, I outline how myth acts as an unquestioned framework behind public understandings. The chapter's conclusion indicates that this unquestioned framework runs counter to the accepted fundamentals of academic economics.

The following three chapters move from the public to the institutions that are responsible for informing and educating the populace about the economy. They indicate how, in different ways and in different forms, the same myth circulates at these centres of power.

Chapter 2 explores the vision of the economy in the financial sector. It begins by outlining how important the financial sector is, not only in its capacity to shape the material conditions of our society, but also with the 'soft power' it wields in its ability to influence public discourse about the economy. Based on the time I spent visiting London's financial district and talking to its inhabitants,[2] the chapter outlines how the sector operates on flimsy, hollow and self-serving representations of knowledge, before concluding by pointing to the type of economic myth that stems from this institutional context, and showing how it pollutes public discourse.

Chapter 3 shifts from the financial to the political sphere and is based on trips I made to Whitehall to speak with civil servants working on economic policy.[3] The chapter first provides some context by indicating the importance of economic communication in the political sphere as well as the civil service's role in economic policy and communication. It then draws on my visits to Whitehall to outline the pressure to present economic knowledge in the political sphere as objective – when it is anything but – and describes the type of myth that stems from this pressure. Finally, before concluding, the chapter provides a case study that looks at how the argument constructed plays out in practice, through the setting of an economic policy: the minimum wage.

Chapter 4 looks at the media as a place that is supposed to form a bridge between the elite sites explored in the previous two chapters (finance and politics) and the 'everyday' people in chapter 1. The chapter starts by outlining the democratic role of the media and its importance in educating the public about the economy and holding elites to account. Having established the media's importance, the chapter moves on to an ethnography of a financial magazine and the many conversations I had with people working in economic journalism.[4]

The interview material and ethnographic observations show that the media promotes a self-serving vision of the economy that aids the myth stemming from the other elite spaces I visited.

While chapters 2, 3 and 4 show the how the institutions that inform and educate the public about the economy are deeply compromised, chapter 5 gives the lie to the myth by dealing with some fundamentals of how our economy actually works. It shows what is wrong with the visions of the economy exposed in the previous four chapters, before concluding on a hopeful note, showing how it is possible to achieve a better future if we are able to dispel the paralysis of myth.

1

Anger, confusion and the pot of money myth

Anger

Tracy lights another cigarette, leans forward on her crinkled faux leather sofa, and with the satisfaction of someone succumbing to an irresistible swell of righteous anger, tells me:

> Rich wealthy men decide what goes where, what we get, what we don't get, what gets spent, where it gets spent and how it gets spent. That's our economy really; it's not in the hands of the people that pay their taxes. It's always been like that: rich, white men.

Gesticulating through the haze of smoke, she continues:

> You've got all these rich snobby idiots up in parliament that don't want to lose out on what they've got, so they punish us for it.

I prompt back: 'So you think they know what they're doing?'

> Oh they know exactly what they're doing. I'm not racist, my kids are mixed race. But they're opening

> the doors to all these foreign people, they're given houses, they're given furniture, they're given this that and the other. And then you've got someone that was born and bred here, I worked until I became ill, and now I have to basically beg for my little bit of money. They know exactly what they're doing! My mum's one of them pensioners that's looking at cuts. My mum is 77, she started working from the age of 10. I think she's entitled to her money, and I think if they took some of their own pay cuts they wouldn't have to tax us so much. Because, trust me, they could still live very comfortably on a quarter of what they earn, no more bonuses, no more taxis, no more hotels, you go and stay in a hotel you pay for it yourself, you pay your own bar bills. What did they do that's any different than an everyday person that works?!

Me, appealing to the logic of democracy: 'But why is that? They get voted in, so someone must have faith in them?'

> Oh we won't even go there! The day you show me a true ballot that's gone through and hasn't been fixed! I'm 46 years of age. I've been voting since I was 16, I've talked to people ... It's fixed from start to finish. They put in who they choose to put in!

Tracy's diatribe was remarkable only in how common the sentiments she expresses are. I'd had hundreds of other conversations with people in Tracy's neighbourhood who, like Tracy, understand the economy as, essentially, a sham. Politics is a charade, the media are full of shit, and it's all orchestrated by rich, white men.

When speaking with Leo, as we were standing on a small patch of grass in his estate's central square I became distracted by his Rottweiler, who crouched beside us to uncurl an enormous stinking mess. But Leo didn't notice; talking about the economy was getting him worked up. In what was becoming a familiar scene, my interviewee began to lose himself in anger. He leant in towards me, as if he'd finally decided to tell me what he really thought, and, in relation to Jeremy Corbyn (leader of the opposition at the time), said:

> Do you know what they'll do, they'll kill him. That's not a word of a lie. I honestly believe that, if he actually gets too close to becoming Prime Minister they will kill him. I do not put it past these people, because these are the same kind of people that killed fucking Kennedy … They will not let him in. Just like the way they fucking killed off Diana.

Des, an experienced youth worker, paused during his lunch break to chat with me on a bench. Between mouthfuls, he drew on a particularly strong version of the prison-industrial complex to explain economic policy. He told me:

> They know what they're doing, and I think they're doing it so they can create more young criminals and put more young people in prisons and so-forth, because prisons pay for these societies. Prisons, for them, is big business, so if we get a lot of young

> boys in the penal system and give them all hardship then when they come out and there's nothing there for them, they're going to carry on the hardship, and get in more trouble. The government is criminalising young people on purpose. They're making them into criminals.

Blatant election riggers, murderers and orchestrators of a penal system based on the principles of slavery were typical representations of the ruling elite in the neighbourhood. Perhaps because I had been cocooned in my university world, where we like to think we're the only ones really sticking it to 'the man', I was surprised by the extent of vitriol towards the establishment.

The estate where Tracy and her neighbours lived is one of the biggest in the UK and was a two-minute walk from where I was living in North London. On days when I wasn't teaching or didn't need to be at university for some other reason, I would head to the estate and talk to people about the economy.

On one of these trips, I met Bryony as she waited on a wall outside a council administration office for a friend to finish work. She was in her late twenties and had just started working as a receptionist in a trendy table-tennis bar after a long period on the dole. After a few questions about how she saw the economy, I saw that familiar anger rise up:

> They will quite happily change the law and the system to suit themselves, without telling us. Quite happily! And then they'll make a speech in parliament, and the average person isn't aware

> of how the system works, but these people have been bred to do this sort of thing so they know the system, they know how it works, how to cheat the system, how to change the system, and how to do it to suit themselves.

Stephanie was a mother of three whom I met queuing in the corner shop. I asked if she thought it was possible to affect economic policy. She frowned and told me:

> Talking's talking, it doesn't actually change what the government does, does it? You can say all these things, but they're going to do what they want to do in the end. They don't listen to people.

Later, as we talked in her front room, I asked her how she would try to explain what the economy was to someone who had no idea, like a child. She responded:

> The economy is good for rich people, but if you're working-class people then it's not good for you. They're just people that sit in the Houses of Parliament, that's about it really, isn't it? You vote for someone on polling day and that's about it. You could vote for anybody and the same person's going to get in no matter what you vote for! So it's just for people that stay drinking tea in the big Houses of Parliament!

Steve, a thoughtful caretaker whom I chatted to over coffee in a local café, shared that view:

> It's for the rich people the economy really. It's about control; I think people at the top always want to

> control the people at the bottom, especially in this country, where we have an exaggerated class system.

These short quotes are chosen from hundreds of conversations about the economy I had with people on the estate. They are typical. Talking about the economy would inevitably lead into a discussion about how the ruling elite used their control of the system for their own benefit while screwing the rest of us over.

It was a small sample and, because of the nature of the area, I was talking mainly to people who had suffered most at the hands of the government's austerity policy. However, the rise in popularity of anti-establishment politics, most obviously evident in the UK by the Brexit vote, indicates that it wasn't just people on this estate who feel this way. Populism has become an accepted byword for the anger, resentment and rejection towards elites that has shaken established democracies in recent years. What my conversations showed was that a large part of this anger concerned how the economy was run, and who it was run for.

So, the first thing to note when trying to get a grip on contemporary public understandings of the economy and the myths that underpin them in the UK, is a widespread mistrust and hatred of the people who are seen to run it. This is important to the story I want to tell, as it undermines that idea that the masses are tricked by the myths of a shadowy elite. Economic myth does emanate from elite institutions, but it is not as simple as the gullible public lapping up the fables told to them by their masters.

Confusion and the pot of money myth

Along with anger, there was also a sense of confusion among the people I spoke to about how the economy works. However, it would be unfair to think that it was just the people on this estate who struggle with the basics of how our economy functions.

Indeed, I was first confronted with my own terrible lack of knowledge on the economy when the global markets crashed in 2008. Compared to most people I ought to have been well equipped: I have an A-level in economics, took economics courses as an undergraduate, read the highbrow press and regularly conversed with the *informed*, whose views, like mine, were shaped by the latest political commentary.

However, when the crisis struck, I had no idea what was going on. I remember being glued to the news channels as I paced my parent's sitting room, muttering to my girlfriend: 'This is big! This is big, really big, you don't understand, this is huge.' I was clueless, but I knew something historic was happening. There were suddenly a million questions I wanted to find the answers to, big questions like: where had all that money gone? Where had all that money come from? If everyone was in debt, who did they owe the money to? Who was to blame? And how could something so intangible be so important? I also had some more practical smaller questions, such as what are derivatives, options, securities, shadow banks, reserve ratios, Euro Dollars, subprime loans? It was as though I had been living in the dark and someone had just switched the lights on and the new world I saw around me, the real world, was utterly confusing.

In the years following the crisis I began trying to educate myself about the workings of our economy. The reading I did allowed me to glimpse some significant truths about how our society works but, without any real prior knowledge, it took a long time to develop a deeper understanding.

Do you, your friends or family know the difference between fiscal and monetary policy? How quantitative easing works? What the Bank of England does? How money is created? If you do, congratulations, but there is a wealth of research to suggest that you are very much in the minority: only 38%[1] of the UK's public understand what inflation is, while 60% cannot select the correct definition of GDP (gross domestic product) from a multiple-choice question,[2] and 70% don't know what quantitative easing (QE) is.[3] Another poll indicates that 85% of MPs don't know how money is created.[4] These are vital aspects to how our economy, and ultimately our society, functions, but as the figures above indicate, they are poorly understood across society.[5]

Asking random people on the estate how they felt about QE or inflation seemed like a sure-fire way to shut any conversation down. So, rather than asking direct questions about the economy, I started asking broader questions like: *how would you explain what the economy was to a child*? This approach brought out a different kind of confusion in the responses I received. Rather than indicating a lack of knowledge over the terminology and the mechanical functioning of our economy, I got a glimpse into what lies behind people's common-sense opinions and views.

And as I spoke to more and more people it became evident that one assumption was dominating and framing how the people I spoke to thought about the economy. I took to calling this 'the pot of money' myth. It was pervasive in almost all my conversations, but was most clearly expressed through the notion of immigrants or refugees subtracting from the national pot.

Sandra, a grandmother who talked to me in a medical centre's waiting room as she and her grandson waited to be seen, even used the pot metaphor. She told me:

> They've let too many refugees in really. There's not enough for the true English people. They've got to think of their own in the country, people that have been paying taxes and things like that before they bring other people in. I mean, I feel sorry for the refugees, but there again, you can't feel sorry for everybody. You've got to help our country, we've got people living here who have to go to the food bank ... they've let so many immigrants in they don't know what to do, they haven't got enough money in the pot to give them.

I spoke to Kelly while she was tending to her garden on a sunny Wednesday afternoon. She told me:

> Here in this block of flats nobody works, I'm the only person that works, so I'm the only person that pays rent. How's that fair? And most of these people are not even from this country, so I just

> don't think that they should be getting it ... I used to be going work at 4 o'clock in the morning when my daughter was only a baby and then working till 6 o'clock at night, while these people were sitting in a warm house getting benefits.

Subi, whom I chatted to in a voluntarily run second-hand clothes shop, was concerned about sovereign debt and foreign aid:

> This country is in so much debt, and part of that debt is by sending foreign aid. I'm not saying we shouldn't help these people but we shouldn't be spending as much on them as we are on our people. We need to sort out this country, there are people who are working two full-time jobs and they've got families, they've got kids and they're still going clothing banks, they're still going food banks.

Linking it to his Jamaican heritage, Des saw the economy as something that people worked hard to build up and contribute to in the post-war years, but was now being taken advantage of and emptied by lazy immigrants. Like the quotes above, the pot of money motif is heavily present in his vision:

> When my parents came over ... they didn't know nothing about handouts, they worked and they didn't come here because they were refugees they came here because the country asked them, begged them to come and help their mother country, to clean up after the war. So they didn't come here

> because they wanted a better life, they came here because this country, the government of England said to them look, we are your mother country, please come and help us, bring your skilled men, we need you to come and build up the economy. Once the economy was built up they started to say 'Well we don't really need you no more', the Jamaicans came here and they done a lot of hard work and look at what's happening now, they're stopping them from coming into the country, and they're part of the commonwealth. I mean that can't be right can it? ... That's what we see, and other people who didn't do as much who didn't participate in the war, just because they're Europeans they can come in and get all the benefits without having put in a stroke of work.

One grey November day I attended a coffee morning at a local community centre. White fold-up tables were placed around a small hall with floor-to-ceiling windows that looked out onto the estate's central square. The garish overhead lighting contrasted with the grey morning sky, and November drizzle rolled across the window panes. I made myself a cup of tea and pretended to browse a table scattered with leaflets, whilst thinking about how to approach the table of laughing elderly women on the other side of the hall. They were the only other people there, so if I was going to talk to someone about the economy, it had to be them. I put my backpack down and approached: 'Hello ladies'. After a little bit of flirty banter with the 'nice young man', they agreed to answer some of my questions and the conversation got going.

The four women had all lived on the estate for more than fifty years and had worked in various jobs since they left school at 15. They were the only people who attended the coffee morning regularly, and liked to set the world to rights over their tea and coffee.

Each of the women hated those in power and blamed the state of society on immigration. The conversation often turned towards lazy yobs or immigrants, and I've quoted it at length as it is a good example of how the pot of money myth dominates everyday understandings of the economy:

Jean (Je), Joyce (J), Irene (I), Terrie (T), W= (when it wasn't clear who was talking or when they were all talking together)

Me: Do you ever talk about the economy or the economic situation

W: No.

T: We don't know what it is so we can't talk about it if we don't know what it is!

Me: What about tax?

W: Yeah it's too high.

I: Things like council tax, that's the only tax we have because none of us work anymore. So we don't pay income tax. But I used to hate it.

Je: That's what they do, see, when I was working for 18 years I paid two full stamps. And then once I retired, and I was still working, they add your pension onto your earnings. They tax the two, so you're working for nothing. That's what I know about tax, and it pisses me right off!

T: How comes they're taking tax off my company pension again? When I was working.

Jo: They do that with your savings as well.

T: It's all economy, there you go!

Je: I don't like economy then!

Me: And what about the minimum wage?

T: It's disgusting, it's too low!

W: It's too low!

[Someone asks how much it is.]

Je: I wouldn't get out of bed for that. But you've got to think of when you left school, you didn't get an overload. So these kids need to learn that they can't get out of bed at three in the afternoon and go and do a job for £20 an hour, that's not how it works, they're going to have to learn.

W: Yeah.

Je: When they're lying in bed to twelve or two it's easy to go down the bank, it's easy for them to go down the bank and get your money out, taking out what I paid in to lay in bed till twos and threes. I've never laid in bed till twos and threes in my life. So all the tax I've paid over the years, to keep the likes of these, even my own! I'm not going to talk about everybody else's, I've got grandchildren that don't want to get out of bed. You know what I mean! So I'm not talking about other people, I'm talking about my own. You want it, go and bleedin' work for it! That's what I'll say to them.

T: If you want to live you've got to work.

Je: Go and get out of bed and bleeding work for it, because I ain't giving it to you!

[...]

Je: I think the country's in a state to be honest with you. There is no more Great Britain and there never will be. What they're allowing to come in, it's costing the country a small fortune. This is a tiny island. Not a massive great big country.

T: All the money that we're paying them [immigrants] is what we're giving!

Je: It's getting worse, it's literally getting worse! And when they try to say to people, have you got spare rooms to take in a big family of Syrians. No! It ain't happening, not in my bleeding house!

Je: Yeah but they're not in their back yards! It's like they let them all in and what happens is your rent goes up. I pay full rent on my flat, I pay full rent, but they put my rent up every year because you've got millions of them that don't pay any rent at all and since they're all coming in they're getting free housing, everything. So therefore, the economy is going to go nutty ... the country's sinking lower and lower.

Me: And you think it's because of the immigration?

W: Yeah that's right.

I: All in all it's down to the government isn't it?

Me: But why do you think the government are doing it?

I: Well because they're letting everything happen. They aren't thinking about us, born and bred here, we've paid our bit. We've paid for the country, so they don't worry about that. They worry about what they've got from other people.

Je: These MPs they can afford it, we can't.

I: And as Jean said, it's costing our country so much money, and where are they getting the money from if it's not from us?

The women's views chime with the notion of the economy as a 'pot of money', something that can be paid into and taken out of. This is evident in how they talk about immigration, through the idea that immigrants are taking out what other people had paid in. It's also there in the idea that the lazy youth are living off the money that the women's generation had paid in through tax.

It's easy to understand where this vision comes from. It is the narrative that has long been used by politicians and the media to justify spending cuts, but more importantly, in the context of people on the estate, it is the narrative that fits most keenly with everyday experience. These citizens see themselves as competing with those around them for scarce resources such as jobs and housing, because they are, in each local context, competing for these resources. So, it makes perfect sense to view the economy as something like a pot that can be filled up and emptied.

When I asked Mic, an out-of-work labourer, why he thought immigration was the most important economic issue of our time, he looked at me as if I were stupid:

If I got a job as a labourer I'd want 60–70 pounds a day minimum. If I was doing it without the

> benefits I'd want 120 pound a day. But these Muppets [immigrants] will do it for 20 quid a day. So they're giving all the jobs to them, ain't they?!

The logic of scarcity: there's only a certain amount of money in the pot so there's only a certain number of jobs, and if we have to share these jobs with more people, and have to share the money which has been put aside for housing and benefit support with more people, it will be bad for us and bad for the economy. This logic is the unquestioned 'prefabricated interpretation' behind how we understand our economy; it is the foundational myth.

The study by ethnographer Anna Killick (2020)[6] into the differences between middle- and working-class understandings of the economy shows this view is shared across a wider spectrum of society than simply those in lower socio-economic groups. And other research, which has been carried out on a far greater scale, demonstrates how widespread the pot of money myth is. In 2017 a nationwide project called *Framing the Economy* found that:

> People saw the economy as functioning like a national pot, with people putting in (contributing) or taking out (draining) … At a societal level, the goal is to keep the pot full. At an individual level, being a responsible member of society means not taking out more than you put in.[7]

Another report,[8] which sought to understand attitudes to the economy among 5,000 members of the public, found that the most common mental model used to picture the economy was as an entity that is added to and subtracted from by groups and individuals putting money in and taking money out.

So, from looking at other research it became clear that the vision underpinning the understanding of the economy held by those people I was talking to was not that different from the fundamental view that underpins visions of the economy across society, that is, as something that is finite and can be paid into or subtracted from – something like a pot of money.

Economics 101

There are implications that stem from viewing the economy as a 'pot of money'. The vision distracts from the institutional structures that shape how society functions; instead, it demonises or praises individuals and groups who are seen as paying in or taking out from the national pot. It's also a vision that limits political and economic imagination by binding us to the idea that we are always restricted by the amount of money in the pot, and that we should always be looking to 'balance the budget'. Furthermore, it does not concur with the reality of how our economy functions.

The first point to make is that governments, as well as private banks, create money out of nowhere. We will discuss this at length later in the book but, given this fact, the idea that there simply *isn't enough money in the pot* doesn't make sense. Money can always be printed, or typed – another zero can always be added.

So, while the aim for individual households and businesses might be to bring in as much money as possible, a nation's economy is a different entity altogether.

Not only can money be magicked up out of thin air, but, a quick skim of any introductory textbook shows that the agreed-upon foundations behind academic economics presents the economy as something very different to a pot of money.

To understand this, we can look at a 'circular flow' diagram: this is one of the first things taught in introductory economics courses and versions of it can be found in all mainstream 101 textbooks.[9] The version of the circular flow diagram shown in Figure 1 simplifies the economy and imagines that it consists of just individuals and firms: the firms employ the individuals, and the individuals buy the goods the firms produce with the wages the firms pay them. This is self-perpetuating, as the money the firms get from the individuals buying their goods goes back into wages, which are then spent on more goods ...

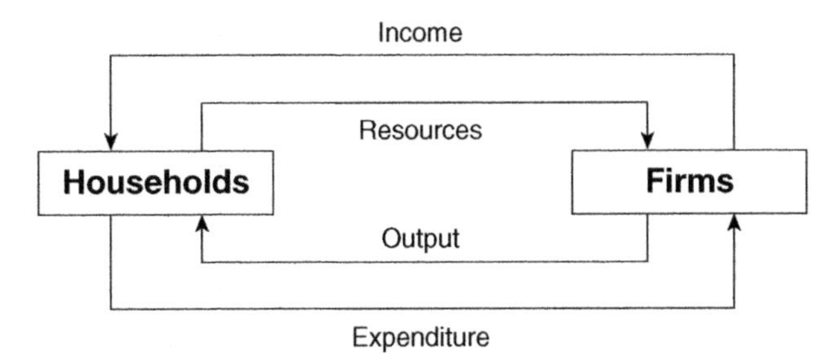

Figure 1 Circular flow diagram

Of course in reality it's a bit more complicated as there are other actors (e.g. the state, the financial sector, other nations' economies), but the basic principle of what it is doesn't change. It is a series of relationships between mutually dependent actors, where money, goods and labour flow in a circular manner. It is not a pot of money that can be filled up and emptied.

What economists disagree on is how this system should be managed. And two approaches have dominated theory and policy for the last hundred years or so. Both of them run counter to the notion of the economy as something akin to a pot of money.

Keynesianism argues that when this system isn't working properly and we have high unemployment – which means individuals don't have the money to buy the firms' output, and everything is starting to slow down – a big dollop of cash introduced by the state can get things moving again. Pouring new money into the system will allow households to buy goods, which will allow firms to employ them again, and the system of mutual dependency kicks back into gear.

However, this cash injection needs to happen when people are unemployed and resources are not already being used. If the system is working fine as it is, and the state just dumps a load of cash on it, all that will happen is that wages will go up along with the price of goods, meaning people will be paid more but everything will cost more – nothing will really have changed. Inflation.

The school of economic theory that took over from Keynesianism and has dominated policy in the past 40 years or so, posits that government spending always leads to inflation. These monetarists argue that left to itself there is a natural balance between the actors in the system, and that adding or taking away money will change none of the fundamental elements (employment or output) but only cause inflation or deflation. For them, the state's role should be to try and keep inflation at a low and stable level in order to avoid the uncertainty and disruption that comes from sudden jumps in prices, and that the state should do this through exercising some control over the amount of money in the system, principally via interest rates.

If the economy was like a pot of money or household budget, policy would be directed towards trying to fill the pot up with as much money as possible. Economic theory would be about working out how best to get money into the pot. However, this clearly isn't the case. States can print money whenever they want to and the great debate in economic theory is about whether or not the state should use its power to add money into the system, or if doing so will only cause inflation.

Drawing out the contrast between public understandings and the basics of economic theory shows how far the pot of money narrative is from reality. It's not just that people don't understand the technical aspects of how our economy works, but that they have an unquestioned fundamental vision of it as one thing, when it is another.

There is myth at play in how we understand our economy.

2

Churches of high finance: myth in the financial sector

Growing up in London in the 1990s it was impossible not to notice the colonisation of certain districts of the city by brash men in sharp suits. Indeed, in the seven or so years it took me to move from having stabilisers on my bike to drinking cider in the park, an entire area of the city was bulldozed over and replaced by towering phallic edifices. On one occasion, when something stronger than cider was coursing through my blood stream, I watched, agog, from the top of a grassy hill as the recently completed tallest building in Europe, Canary Warf, detached itself from its foundations and zigzagged gracefully across the skyline.

The trippy new cityscape and the men in suits had risen off the back of major deregulation in the 1980s. What was once a tightly regulated industry turned into a free for all as, under Thatcher, the movement and provision of credit became the most profitable exercise in British history. By 2019 the total amount of assets owned by the financial sector in the UK was close to £25 trillion.[1] To put it into context, that figure is roughly

300 times the amount of government spending in 2019 (300 years of government spending!).

In a direct way (via loans and investment), banks and other financial firms determine how much money is in the economy and how it is allocated across society. In a less direct way, the sector has considerable power through its ability to influence politics and shape public discourse about the economy.

Official figures show that 51.4% of donations to the Conservative Party in 2010–2011 came from the City of London,[2] while in the build up to the 2019 election it was estimated to be considerably more.[3] Alongside influence through political lobbying, the sector also holds considerable sway in the media. Despite only appealing to a small segment of the population, a third of editorial content in the press is devoted to business and financial news,[4] which is tailored towards the sector and littered with PR[5] from it, making advertising from the City a key source of funding. This influence impacts media coverage,[6] and accusations that both the media and politics have been captured by finance are common in contemporary commentary. This 'soft power' means that finance plays a critical role in shaping government policy and in shaping how the economy is presented to the public at large. As such, it is an important space in the production and dissemination of economic myth.

The institutional context behind the myth

What distinguishes financial capitalism is that wealth is generated by the circulation of signs grounded in a seemingly endless play of signs rather than in the sale or exchange of material objects or physical labour. (Taylor)[7]

XX Victoria street is like a city within a city; there is a café and some shops on the ground floor. The most striking thing is the quantity of space inside the lobby, a waiting area with huge windows all the way round. I sit on one of the low-lying leather sofas in front of an oblong coffee table which has a scattering of magazines aimed at people who own property or enjoy high-octane adventure sports. People are smartly dressed but not all shirts are tucked in. When it's time for the interview I am let through the glass gates that permit access to the lift doors, enter the glass-walled lift and go up to the 9th floor. A sign directs me to the offices of the hedge fund I am here to visit. The companies lobby is all lush green carpet and oak wood, the receptionist directs me to the room where the meeting will take place. It's a small room taken up by a large oak table upon which sits a small china tea set and glass bottles of still and sparkling water. On the walls there are tasteful pictures of Edwardian London. The whole place reverberates with the casual formality of an expensive club. The feeling you get is that this is all here for you and you should behave in a certain way, but it is not a restraining type of formality, the kind I have felt when I have been to exclusive restaurants, but more an empowering one. These things are all there

> for you, the customer; it's more like being welcomed into a posh hotel: these people are here to provide you with a service. (Author's field notes)

Pre-pandemic, one square meter of floor space in central London cost around £19,500,[8] and while sitting in the vast lobbies of the buildings that house the banks and hedge funds I visited I would reflect on the parallels between the aesthetics of these spaces and the institutions themselves. The lobbies are clearly symbols of power. When one is allowed to enter such a space, the contrast with the busy streets outside creates a sense of entitlement – only you and a few others are allowed to enter. But it achieves this effect not through imposing ostentatious symbols of wealth on the visitor, but through the opposite: empty space. It is what is not there, what does not exist that creates this effect of luxury and power, just as the trade that these institutions conduct appears to be based on something that doesn't exist, something that is not there but has the capacity to allocate enormous power – *the capacity to make you rich.*

The symbolism of these spaces must impact upon those who work in the buildings and pass through them every day on the way to their own offices; however, the principal recipients of the lobbies' latent symbolism are clients or potential clients, who wait in these spaces until they are summoned to one of the floors above. The anthropologist Anna Tsing notes the importance of representation in finance:

> In speculative enterprises, profit must be imagined before it can be extracted; the possibility of

> economic performance must be conjured like a spirit to draw an audience of potential investors.[9]

The luxurious meeting offices and the vast lobbies are part of this 'conjuring' – particularly when compared to the open-plan back offices where the employees actually work, which are no different from offices in any other industry.

What about the inhabitants of these spaces? One would have thought from the outside that people working in finance would be dominated by the cold clear logic of money. That finance would be a place where people with razor-sharp minds banish all sentiment and emotion as they hunch over computer screens and interpret numbers you and I will never understand. A place where the bottom line is all that matters. Yet, as I spoke to more and more people, it became evident that in fact, much of the work carried out in the industry is concerned with a softer, more persuasive, more malleable type of logic, one which is explicitly concerned with appealing to sentiment and emotion. A type of logic in which myth can thrive.

When Caroline, an investment manager in her mid-thirties, entered the meeting room, she emanated reassuring, assertive warmth. Carrying a copy of the introduction booklet she presents to the firm's prospective clients, and telling me that she had friends and colleagues she could arrange for me to meet, it seemed clear that she had an eagerness to please. Caroline repeatedly emphasised the importance of personal interaction in her work and explained that, for her, engendering a sense of trust in the client was essential:

> It is all about trust, because I am with private clients. If this were a meeting where you had your pension and you wanted to know should you invest it with us or someone else ... a lot of it is going to be about the person who you meet and if you think you can trust them ... We fall under investment services, so the service we provide is very important.

This sentiment was also expressed by Calum, a wealth manager at a multinational bank. Calum was in many ways the archetype of a certain city stereotype: white, male, somebody who attended a public boarding school from a young age, studied Politics and Economics at a Russell group university and did an internship in the City 'because that's what other people were doing'. He lived in Chelsea and, as he described it, had been funnelled through the system in a particular fashion that seemed to inevitably lead to him working for a major bank.

Yet, after a few beers, he was telling me how he was sick of his job and wanted to change industry. When I pressed him on why, he explained:

> I don't want to do my job because ultimately I couldn't give less of a fuck if Mr Smith is 2% down in his portfolio for a year or 3% up. That is why I don't want to do it anymore.

Such a lack of empathy with the bank's clients and their portfolios would be a major issue in Calum's current role. Calum worked in wealth management, which meant that he helped the bank facilitate bespoke portfolios for the super-rich. When I asked him about the skills I would need to acquire if I were going to perform his job starting from tomorrow, he initially told me it was important to be fairly numerate and have a broad analytical understanding of the products these high net-worth individuals invest in. Then he said:

> But you also need to be a people person because essentially it's a relationships game. You need to be able to speak confidently on a peer-to-peer basis with someone who is, generally speaking, a lot older than you and significantly more successful … Most people normally doing what I do are 45–50, because most ultrahigh net-worth individuals, generically, are white, male and 55 plus.

Just as for Caroline, the central aspect of Calum's role was the cultivation of relationships with customers. As both indicate, these relationships were based on personal encounters between them and their customers, so like any sales person, the type of cultural and symbolic capital they were able to bring to these relationships mattered a great deal in their capacity to attract custom, as did their representation of the institutions and ultimately the industry that employed them.

For Calum, his serious, affable persona, his maleness, and the class he was born into provided him with the foundations upon which he could easily construct the type of personality required to successfully conduct these relationships. For Caroline, her 'front office' role as a fund manager required her to engender clients with trust in her judgement. She readily admitted that this was not achieved by thorough in-depth analysis of 'nitty-gritty detail', but instead through her softer 'people skills'.

The relationships key to roles like Calum and Caroline's jobs require a presentation of economic information as neat, ordered and reliable accounts of the future, which can be summed up and relayed back to customers. Both told me that with customers, they frequently stressed the precariousness of the positions taken by their respective firms and that 'no one can predict the future'; yet their roles were to present themselves as the front of efficient and knowledgeable future-predicting (and therefore money-making) organisations, and as such they needed to imply that their particular organisation may not be perfect, but in terms of its future predictions, it was better than all the others. Key to both their roles is representation: of themselves, of their firms, and ultimately of the knowledge-base that their firms operate under. This representation of knowledge is central to the type of myth generated in the sector, but before we get to that, let's stay with the 'relationships game' a little while longer.

I met Will, an energy broker, after work one spring evening in a pub down a side street close to Sloane Square in Chelsea. He insisted he buy the first round of drinks. He was clearly looking forward to his beer and got through three pints in the hour and a half we spoke. Will was in his mid-to-late thirties. He was heavy-set, with a sardonic manner, but when he spoke he was utterly engaging; it felt like he was opening himself up and giving you everything. It was very hard not to feel charmed by him.

In many ways Will represents a different sort of city stereotype to Calum. He was expelled from school as a teenager but was still 'sharp' enough to attend university, after which he started temping in London and continuing what he called the 'student life'. When a friend, citing his 'gobbiness', suggested he apply for a role at a city firm, he did. They took him on as a 'skivvy', making tea and helping out with the admin. Realising that he needed to stand out if he wanted to join one of the desks he started a betting syndicate based on a popular TV game show, which the whole office would stop to watch at 5pm. Will would act as a bookie going round to different desks taking bets. One of the desks liked his boisterous personality and took him on. He talked about how he was drawn to the glamour of the industry, the expenses-paid trips abroad, the late-night partying and the 'charged' atmosphere in the office. He told me that he would often go out with colleagues, getting to bed at 4am, but then have to be in work a couple of hours later at 6.30. I asked him, did everybody stay out late? What if someone wanted an early night? He simply said: 'No, you couldn't, no one in that job would go home early.'

The type of 'character' Will had was evidently very important in his career progression, but it was also central to his job as a broker, matching buyers and sellers. He called it a 'personality-based job' and his months were broken up into short trips to different cities in Europe and stints entertaining clients in London.

I found it hard to accept that these engagements served no obvious business purpose. When I asked him to explain a bit more about these trips, he told me:

Will: They're to see the clients and make sure they keep on using you, not the other guy.
Me: So it's kind of like a social call?
Will: Very much, it's totally like that, 100%, and your job is to become friends with them. There are loads of people that I see now who started off as clients who I don't deal with any more, they've gone on to do other things or they're just dealing with other people and I still see them regularly as mates, so it's not like 'I'm going to pretend to be your mate'. You quickly cycle through and you say I'm not going to work with this guy but I will work with this guy, he's a more natural fit for me.

I believed Will when he said he didn't pretend to like people in order to become friends with them. Given his gregarious nature, and that it takes a certain type of personality to survive in this particular branch of the industry (i.e. you can't go home early on a night out), he was very much at home with the people he did business with. Interpersonal relationships are vital to the flow of business in Will's world, but these relationships are constructed on whether or not the people are a 'good fit', whether or not they like each other. Shared norms and a shared method of communicating are what matters.

The importance of connections was reiterated by Matthew, who described himself as a 'roving bank director'. Matthew had worked close to the top of some of the major financial institutions in the UK and lionised the 'rainmakers', those special people who can pull off really big deals. When I asked him how he thought they did it, he explained;

> It is often, and I have seen this time and again, it is someone who has the one contact, makes the one phone call and it might have nothing else to do with the deal. People could be labouring long and hard for weeks, whole teams ... and this person says: 'Wait a minute, I know so and so. I saw him last week and he told me he was looking for just this sort of proposition.' That one phone call or one contact can be worth millions of fees.

Rather than the cold hard logic that I had envisioned dominating the financial world, it became clear that, like all service industries, softer 'people skills' were what matters. I stated to realise that in this community, who you know and how persuasive you can be, is at least as important as what you know.

In his book on the financial crisis the psychoanalyst David Tuckett writes about how the crisis was caused by the circulation of narratives which were driven by what he calls 'groupfeel'.[10] This relates to how a tight-knit community can create narratives that shape their thought and govern their behaviour, even if there is no external or objective reason to believe in them. Essentially, what he's saying is that in exclusive communities based around the softer logics of norms and cultural values, shared stories that have little connection to reality can flourish.

The idea of myth becomes prescient in such contexts. Prior to the 2008 crisis people working in finance were not lying to themselves or the world about the situation. It was more, as Tuckett explains, that the shared belief, which underpinned how they understood the world and the narratives they told themselves about their work, became so detached from what was happening, that when reality struck the system crumbled. As a former Cambridge-educated fund manager I met, put it:

> Living through the financial crisis definitely gave me the idea that I didn't know shit about economics and what I learnt in a degree just wasn't worth the paper it was printed on. I had to go back to square one ... you just get abstracted by all the bullshit.

The world within a world

Like many of the older people I spoke with, Oliver had been 'sucked up' into the industry in the early 1980s. Having attended an exclusive school and then Oxford, he thought it might be 'quite fun' to work in the City, and had been employed in various roles. We spoke in late winter beside a warm fire at his Chelsea home, as he reflected on his career:

> You get quite pampered ... At Goldman Sachs, for example, in their basement, they have a whole sort of mall with different places you can eat. There are about eight different cuisines: a sushi bar and

> everything like this. I remember someone explaining to me that the idea was that in the ideal world no Goldman Sachs employee would ever actually have to leave the building because everything was provided. There would be breakfast and lunch served and everything, and you'd get taxis whenever you wanted, and make them wait as long as you wanted. You always flew business class and stayed in very good hotels, and all this sort of thing ... you do get a bit insulated from the real world.

He went on:

> They don't care about the UK economy. They don't really care about this country ... they live in Chelsea and Kensington. They send their kids to expensive schools. They have nannies and skiing holidays, and go to the Hurlingham Club or whatever, and most of their friends are probably international bankers. So they're not integrated, really ... they're not really interested in what's going on in the Conservative Party or Labour Party, or that there's a housing crisis in somewhere or other, because they live in Central London and they travel a huge amount.

This detached social sphere is connected to the type of work conducted in the financial sector, which, socialising aside, is mainly concerned with being aware of and keeping up with others in the community. This is because the market moves depending on what other market actors do, rather than any underlying fundamentals. This has long been an accepted fact about financialised capitalism, as is indicated by the mainstream economist John Kay:

> In markets of today, what matters is not so much knowledge of the economy – knowledge of business, economic development, global politics – as knowledge of the activities of other market participants.[11]

In a community in which the crucial thing is to stay with, and hence predict, the movements of others, the belief that actors hold regarding the beliefs of other market participants, rather than any underlying content, is what matters. Calum (the wealth manager who doesn't give a fuck about his clients' portfolios), reflected on how, in finance, this communal reflexivity holds precedence over any solid forms of information or knowledge:

> The interesting thing ... is that actually there are no fundamentals and it is entirely about the belief structure and therefore if we do panic then it is game over, so that's the paradox ... it's a reflexivity phenomenon.

Shared belief is what counts, regardless of the foundations of that belief. Knowledge about other actors, rather than knowledge grounded in thorough research, is what lies behind action, and fleeting opinions and rumour can matter more than well-researched empirical evidence. As such, both the social world and the actual work that people in the industry conduct are rife with emotional and sentimental logic, with a form of rationale that propels the generation of myth.

Experts and the role of economic knowledge

Given the insular nature of behaviour in financial markets, and that what matters is being one step ahead of the other participants regardless of the underlying factors, I asked Jamie, a younger version of Will (the boisterous broker), why financial institutions pay so many analysts and economists to conduct economic research into these underlying factors. His brow furrowed in response and then, just before tucking into a second lunchtime pint, he offered an interesting but ultimately unsatisfactory answer:

Jamie: Each fund will have a fund manager who makes the actual investment decisions. He'll have portfolio people making sure he's doing everything okay ... he will have a whole host of analysts, who will be researching the market, doing everything they can. These people are like Cambridge-educated a lot of the time, really intelligent people who are looking at the market and feeding back to the fund manager. And then ... it always has to follow the benchmarks, which will be other people's funds, which will be the market itself.

Me: Kind of what you're saying is that despite the whole team who feed this information to the fund manager, the fund manager is probably just going to try and stay with the market, spread it out as much as possible.

Jamie: Yes, pretty much.

In order to spread risk, fund managers frequently invest as broadly as possible so they stay with the market. The rise in passive funds is testament to this.[12] Passive funds are now more popular than active funds,[13] which they have consistently out-performed (passive funds have been four times as profitable since 2007). Passive funds simply track the market index; they just follow the market, as opposed to 'active' funds, in which fund managers make decisions based on their own expert analysis and the analysis of their teams of highly educated analysts.

While my question, 'What is the role of economics and expert advice in the financial sector?', hadn't really been answered in Jamie's response, the most successful financer I spoke to was able to shed some light on the issue.

I met Alex in a coffee shop close to his home in North London. Due to a local charitable initiative and a scholarship, Alex attended one of the UK's elite schools and then studied at Oxford. Upon graduating he was 'hoovered up' by a stockbroker firm as part of the industry's mass intake in the early 1980s. Having established the European arm of a major US hedge fund, he retired in his forties just prior to the 2008 crisis, to 'run' his own money.

Alex spent much of the interview lamenting the short-termism of the financial and political economy and claimed that a large part of this short-termism stemmed from the way knowledge is disseminated. He explained that, given the current regulations, having an information advantage is illegal; thus, all information is open and free for all to view. This leads to a rise in the importance of public predictions made by economic forecasters. Fund managers and analysts know that this information is often ungrounded or misguided but they also know that they must act on it, as others will act on it. So again, here we see how flimsy, short-term and ungrounded information holds sway in the financial community. Furthermore, Alex's testimony gives us a glimpse from an insider's perspective of the role of 'expert analysis' in the financial sector, which appears to be far less solid and substantial than it might look to be from the outside:

> All the economists I've ever really come across are basically pontificators and forecasters of incorrect forecasting – all of them – they might as well be philosophers.

Given that it is now very hard, if not illegal, to have an information edge, and company statements don't tell the whole story, markets move according to information put out in the short term by the economic 'experts' Alex was complaining about. This means that it is harder to take a long-term view on something, as it is difficult to acquire sufficient trustworthy information from firms and – given the volatility of the market, which moves as a result of hearsay and unfounded opinion – even if you *do* take a correct long-term position on something it will be harder to hold that position given that the price could deviate from your prediction in the short term. Furthermore, trades are made daily and you ultimately want to end the day up rather than down, so even if an economic expert makes a statement that you know is inaccurate, you also know that it will move the market, so you act accordingly. Alex explained this process, stating that when he started in the industry he naively believed that other people knew what they were talking about, but soon realised they didn't:

> I think at the start you know nothing, you assume everything. All these people who are much more experienced than you, they know everything. It becomes clear quite quickly that's not the case …
>
> [For instance] every month you'd have nonfarm payrolls. Friday lunchtime, 1:30pm, this figure will come out … An enormous importance was being ascribed to this thing every month, and it's a big consensus forecast … A consensus number … is made up by economists, maybe there's some surveys underlying it, but they've guessed it.
>
> It completely ruined Friday afternoons for a lot of the City because when they really wanted to be down the pub, they had to sit there and wait for this ridiculous number, which had no real relevance but which did actually move markets on a monthly basis on a Friday afternoon, crazy.

Alex went on to tell me about his relief at having retired and no longer having to pay attention to these groundless but market-moving numbers:

> I mean, when I look back on what I did, I ran this portfolio of shares for 13 years, literally looking at

> minute-by-minute moves and how I was doing on the day, and worrying. The moment I walked out of that office, I went, 'How ludicrous is this?' I mean I knew it really, but it became completely clear to me that I no longer cared if something was up 2p on the day. It made no difference.

When I asked Alex how he became successful and what he had learnt in the job, he told me that it was all luck. I protested, pointing out that he was trusted with investing vast sums of money. Surely it can't just have been luck? He responded:

> Oh yes, you pretend to be better at something than others knowing all the time you really don't know anything.

This was something of a surprise, coming from the most senior and successful person I spoke to. The idea that 'it is all just luck' is not a tenable position that Calum or Caroline would be able to hold when they mixed with clients – nor is it one that it is advisable to espouse if you wish to get on with your colleagues and move up in the industry, as was illustrated by the discussions with Will, Matthew and Oliver. Yet Alex, retired and no longer needing to convince people that he knew more than them, didn't mind telling me that his millions were achieved not through his capacity to predict the future better than anyone else, or his capacity to understand complex economic models, but due to luck.

Finally, James, a successful but disillusioned fund manager, seemed to clarify how flimsy the knowledge base in the financial sector is:

> I think working in the financial system makes you realise that beliefs do change through time and how quickly fear and greed can alternate ... Because if you see the world through the eyes of the people who are supposedly the big decision-makers, the guys who are determining things, and you see the way their version of the world is so very simplistic and wrong, it makes you definitely think well, Christ! What if the politicians don't understand either?

In the financial sector, economic knowledge doesn't need to be grounded in anything deeper than symbolic representations of truth. As long as the knowledge is believed, or it is believed that others believe it, or (more likely) it is believed that others will believe others believe it (*ad infinitum*), it has the capacity to move markets, cause outcomes, and make someone money.

Such a shallow epistemological grounding contributes to the notion of the financial sector as a community organised around flimsy representations of knowledge. If we combine this shallow epistemological grounding with the insular social world described by Oliver, we see that finance is a detached realm held together through loose representations of knowledge, and, as such, it is an industry in which myth can thrive.

Myth in the City

Writing in the 1960s the influential sociologists Peter Berger and Thomas Luckmann developed the notion of 'reification'.[14] This is analogous to Dr Frankenstein and his monster, as it relates to the idea that the things we create take on an agency and power of their own.

However, there is one crucial difference. With the concept of reification, the good doctor never loses control over his monster, it's just that he convinces himself that he does. And it is this notion of reification – that we believe the things we create and control take on their own agency – that is at the core of myth in the financial sector.

First, the economy is separated out from other human endeavours and presented as a de-politicised, autonomous entity. Then, once it has been detached from the world of human agency, the next step occurs, and the economy, separated out from other human endeavours, takes on the form of a finite set of resources or a 'pot of money'.

Step 1: the economy as a de-politicised autonomous entity

Having spent some time talking to them, it became evident that people in finance draw a clear distinction between politics and the economy. The world of politics was limited to human decision making and power relations, whereas 'the economy' was separate from the human world and followed its own logic. As Rebeca, a fund manager told me:

> What frustrates me is that politicians can never admit that they don't really have any control ... So they take credit for when the economy is growing really fast and then people try and put blame on it when it goes in the other direction.

And Will, a broker, stated:

> Nothing that they [politicians] do will ever change anything, because all of it is made up by so many tiny individual twitches in a vast massive twitch.

When talking about whether or not austerity is a political or economic issue, Matthew (the roving bank director) explained:

> I don't call it politics; I think it's just telling the truth. Politicians aren't very good at this, but it does come down to telling the truth.

The quotes above demonstrate the idea that the economy operates under a separate logic to politics. There is a notion that political logic is flawed and subject to human fallibility when compared to a more powerful, fundamental driving force that steers the economy. Distinguishing between political and economic agencies has the effect of de-politicising the economy, which is seen to operate according to a baser and more essentialised logic than political logic. Emphasising a vision of the economy as an autonomous driving force in this way acts as a legitimation mechanism; it masks the role the financial sector plays in the unequal distribution of wealth across society, and by mystifying the economy it provides a platform for the claims to knowledge discussed earlier in the chapter.

It is also possible to understand the myth of a depoliticised economy as being grounded in the type of labour conducted in the industry. Much of the work in the sector revolves around predicting the movement of, and seeking out patterns in, numbers on computer screens – numbers which represent the economy. As the actors admit, a fool-proof model of the economy is impossible; however, they have to present it as a system that, if it cannot be worked out, can at least be partially understood or mapped, so that they will be able to make more money out of it than the next person. These factors further encourage a sense of the economy as a reified autonomous system that is detached from everyday reality:

> It's just all about getting it done. You don't think, 'Oh, it's so great that they're building a new factory in China, and it's going to provide 10,000 jobs for the Chinese' ... Occasionally you go and visit a factory and put on a hard hat, and do a lot of nodding, without understanding anything that the factory manager is telling you. We used to make jokes about it: 'Oh, that is a big one. I've never seen one that size before!' But it's pretty far removed. (Oliver, former analyst)

> There is nothing that I have ever seen which is actually real in any of my time doing my 10 years of work. (Tom, city based accountant)

> Financial markets are an enormous game of chess in the sky, which is why no one will ever really master it. (Jackson, Former Broker)

If we think that day in day out, city workers need to apply some kind of framework that helps them understand this abstract world, it's easy to see how a type of reification might occur. This is because they need to objectify this abstract system in order for it to become an object which they can claim to have knowledge of.

As such, the abstract nature of the phenomena they are looking at on a daily basis, combined with the need for them to present themselves as knowledgeable, contributes to the sense of this phenomena existing independently – to its reification. And once it has been reified in this manner, human or political agency are no longer properties of the object in question (the economy), leading to Will's conclusion that 'Nothing that they [politicians] do will ever change anything'.

Therefore, it is possible to link the de-politicisation of the economy as an abstract autonomous entity to the notion of the financial sphere as a community centred around loose representations of knowledge. As I have argued here, the need for there to be something about which to have knowledge over is critical to the functioning of the City, regardless of the foundations of that knowledge. As such, the reproduction of a mythological economy that reifies it as an autonomous depoliticised entity provides people working in the City with an object that they can claim specialist knowledge of.

Step 2: the economy as a 'pot of money'

Reifying the economy as a de-politicised abstract entity facilitates the next step in how the economy is mythologised in the financial sector, as by separating it out as a distinctive sphere it becomes possible to conceive of it as something akin to a pot of money – which we do not have full control over, but, like a household budget, we can add to and spend.

There are two principal ways this myth manifests itself in the City: 1) the idea that there is a certain amount of money in the economy and that the financial sector is the best way to allocate it across society (spending); and 2) the idea that the profit made by those in the sector contributes to a 'pot of money' by creating value and helping to pay for the rest of society (adding to the pot). Both these ways of thinking about the economy are made possible through the notion of the economy as a depoliticised autonomous entity.

The financial sector as the best way to spend the 'pot of money'

This is the myth that the financial sector provides a service to society by helping the market function and allocating money in the most efficient and productive manner possible:

> I feel like I'm efficiently allocating capital to businesses. I genuinely feel that that's true. I'm part of that process where money flows to the right businesses. (Felix, quantitative analyst)

> It is facilitating the flow of money. You're conscious of that to some degree. Not personally when you're sitting at your desk lobbing some shares around, that's not going to do a great deal, but you're conscious that the system is doing that. (Alex, former fund manager)

The myth that the financial sector carries out an important function for society by allocating capital to the places that will use it most efficiently and thus produce value, allowing the investors a better return, is a foundational legitimation of the sector's role in society.[15] Behind it is the idea that finance acts as an intermediator between savers and companies: people who want to save money and earn a bit of interest place their money with banks or investment firms and then those firms lend out this money to companies who employ people and make things. As such, in this vision, there is a certain amount of money in the economy, and finance's role is to spend that money most efficiently: a virtuous circle ensues, as savers get interest and firms receive investment, and the bankers get paid.

There are a number of reasons why, in our contemporary context, this position is hard to maintain: the principal one, discussed in detail later in the book, is that major financial institutions create money rather than act as intermediators in the allocation of capital and, as I will show, this renders the 'pot of money' metaphor redundant.[16] Furthermore, only 3% of the money invested/created by the financial sector goes to the production of goods and services, with the majority of it being used for speculation and other unproductive purposes;[17] this statistic makes a mockery of the 'best allocation of resources' myth.

However, our purpose here is not to undermine the views held in the financial sector (see chapter 5), but to try and discern the notion of the economy that lies at the base of these views. The 'best allocation of resources' myth sees the economy as something akin to a 'pot of money' that needs to go somewhere: money exists and it needs to be allocated across society in the best possible fashion. This myth serves to legitimise the role of the sector in society and justify the claims to knowledge made across the industry. This is because, through their expertise and the market logic that they obey, financial services are seen to be able to seek out the best investments and allocate capital in the most efficient manner possible, not just for their customers but for society as a whole.

The financial sector adds to the pot of money

I met Matthew, the 'roving bank director', at his large town house in North London. He initially seemed a little flustered and impatient, as he was flying to Russia that afternoon, but soon he lost himself in the conversation and we ended up talking for close to two hours. After I explained a little bit about what I had been doing, he asked me whether or not I had found much anti-banker sentiment amongst the 'everyday' people I had spoken to. When I told him that a lot of people harboured considerable resentment towards the financial sector, he looked pained and told me:

> But about 3% of people in this country pay for the other 97%. Actually that is not quite true about 10% or something break-even. I can't remember the figures, but about 3% basically pay for everyone else except for the people who are economically neutral. It is a fact, it is simply a fact.

Matthew's lament was the clearest illustration of this particular vision of the economy, a vision that was frequently expressed by many of the City workers I spoke to. Underlying this narrative is the notion often expounded by the media and politicians that British society relies on the City because the tax revenues collected from the amount of money made there can then be allocated to the places that need it (e.g. the NHS or schools) or to the people that are not capable of earning enough. Underpinning this idea is the myth of the economy as a finite 'pot of money', something that is added to and taken away from. Some people (Matthew and colleagues) place money into the pot through their value-creating activity, and some people (those on council estates) take money out. It is a very simple and clearly defined vision of what the economy is.

If money's creation and allocation is determined by major private financial institutions (as I will show later), then the idea that people working in these institutions reap money from their hard toil, and use that money to pay for the rest of society, doesn't add up. Like the monarchs who ruled societies of old, their power stems from their structural position within the broader social sphere, and the capacity to create money out of nothing.

However, even if we discount how money is created and subscribe to Matthew's 'pot of money' myth, it is worth considering that in 2008 $700 billion was released by congress to rescue the US banking system,[18] and in the UK the Bank of England released £500 billion to save the banks.[19] The corporation tax collected from the financial services over the past 30 years has varied from around £4 billion to £13 billion[20] a year. These figures[21] pale into insignificance if we think about the scale of the bailout, and are a drop in the ocean if we compare them to the UK's total tax revenue, which in 2020 was £828 billion.[22]

So, even if it were a simple case of money going in and out of a finite system, the banks have pushed far more out than they have put in. But it is also important to remember that the money used to bail out the banks was not taken from tax revenues but invented by central banks, in the same way that private banks invent money daily.

Underlying the belief outlined above is the 'absurd proposition'[23] that profit equals value. The idea that 'if we are making money what we are doing is valuable' feeds the self-entitlement behind this vision. It makes possible the notion that high earners generate profit from valuable toil, thus adding to the 'pot of money', which is then reinvested to create economic growth, with a section of it being used up by the lazy or incapable, who create nothing of value themselves.

Different strands of this 'common-sense' view of how the economy functions were harboured by almost all of the people I spoke to who worked in finance. One example is David, who was in his early thirties and came from the Home Counties. Despite various attempts to get into the City he ended up working in administration. As an administrator he dealt with businesses that went under and was far removed from the big money earned in the City, yet through talking to him it became clear that he revered the City elites that he still wished to join someday:

> These guys work their whole life really hard. These are guys who are working all the time. You get these top guys, Goodwin or whatever, 'Fred the Shred', you see the end of his career. He's 50 or 60 years old and he's getting paid a fortune. This guy has worked his arse off over the last 40 years. You'll get someone who is like, 'It's awful.' [But] It's like, well, this guy is at the top of his game, he's worked his arse off. He probably deserves it.
>
> The economy – what's the word – re-governs itself ... These guys are doing really difficult jobs, really seriously difficult. Jobs that people just would sit there and be like, 'No idea how to do this.' These guys have done it. They've managed to get to that. It's not a coincidence.

David's belief in the divine justice of the economy through its capacity to 're-govern itself' by rewarding those who contribute to it by producing profit equates to the notion that profit is value: it's 'not a coincidence' that these people are earning lots of money; they must 'deserve it', as the economy 're-governs' itself by rewarding those who contribute by adding value. The applicability of this view of financial services depends upon the idea that money and profit are created through value-creating activities, therefore those who earn money must be adding value to society and thus deserve the rewards they reap from their labour. In this simplistic myth, 'the economy' is understood to be something like a collective piggy bank: those creating value contribute to it and rightfully get something back according to what they put in, because as a depoliticised system, the economy rewards value creators.

The brash men in sharp suits who had changed the skyline of the city I grew up in did not adhere to the views I previously held about them. Instead of the steely cold logic that I envisioned dominating the huge office blocks at the centre of twenty-first-century capitalism, I found a soft core. Representation, persuasion and myth are at the heart of what drives the community in the financial sector.

This soft core is a place where the type of narratives and groupfeel Tuckett writes about can easily take hold, and as such, it is a place where myth can triumph over reality. Due to finance's ability to shape 'who gets what and what goes where', bend politics to its will, and dictate representations of the economy in the media, we ought to pay attention to the type of myth created there.

Firstly, a vision of the economy that depoliticises it by reifying it as an entity operating according to its own autonomous logic removes human agency. Since human actors are understood as merely complying with the irresistible base force that drives the economy rather than dictating it, the un-egalitarian manner in which the financial sector creates and distributes wealth (as demonstrated later in the book) is masked by the myth of the economy as an autonomous force.

Secondly, conceiving of the economy as a depoliticised entity helps facilitate the pot of money myth, which allows finance to claim that it is best placed to allocate capital (spend), and that, through the value it creates by paying into the pot (through tax), it should receive the highest rewards. As such, the pot of money myth cuts through the vision of the economy in the sector and allows those working there a justification for their elevated social and economic status.

However, the upfront costs of the bailout in 2008 were equivalent to over 10 years of total taxes collected from the sector,[24] and the longer-term impact of the crisis has been calculated at a far, far higher cost of around £1.8 trillion.[25] So even if it was a case of money going in and out of a system, the financial sector would be heavily in debt to the state and the rest of society. So much for the idea that the sector pays its way through tax.

As for the notion that finance allocates resources in the most effective and efficient fashion, I again refer you to the fact that only around 3% of the money issued by the sector goes to firms that make goods or provide services – firms that benefit the broader economy. Indeed, researchers who attempted to quantify the cost of this gross misallocation of resources calculated that from 1995 to 2015 finance cost the UK 2.7 trillion.[26]

So, even if we understand finance on its own terms, it is evident that the narratives circulating in the financial community as self-justifications for its power do not correspond with reality. However, important as totting up a cost benefit analysis might be, it is more valuable to think of the role of finance as an actor in a broader system. An actor which smiles while it drains the lifeblood out of its fellow actors and out of the system itself.

3

Magic money tree: myth in the political sphere

It would be hard to overstate how important economic narratives have become to governments and political parties. These narratives, and the myths that they are founded upon, can justify key policy shifts and win or lose elections.

Consider the 'magic money tree' rhetoric, which was used to great effect in the 2017 and 2019 general elections. The population was relentlessly told, first by Theresa May and then by Boris Johnson, that if elected, Labour's reckless policies would bankrupt the nation; that there is no magic money tree, and that Labour's promise to increase government spending and support the welfare state was a load of pie in the sky nonsense, which cuts against the fundamental laws that govern our economy.

The rhetoric rested upon, and possibly succeeded because of, a vision of the economy that has been at the centre of state communication for a decade – that the nation's pot was emptied by the feckless spending of New Labour in the late 1990s and 2000s, and that following this, the state needed to cut back on intervention and welfare spending in order to save money and create a leaner more productive economy – as only through such austere measures could we hope to fill the pot back up again.

This vision is a pure form of the pot of money myth, and was the almost unchallenged view of the economy in the political sphere between 2010 and 2020. Then, in early 2020 the pandemic struck. Great swaths of the economy were forced to close and suddenly, facing mass civil unrest and the breakdown of society, the Chancellor, Rishi Sunak, found the magic money tree.

Of course, if you had been paying close attention, it would have been obvious that it was there all along and was already in use through the quantitative easing programme. But in 2020 the magic money tree became public knowledge, as the state simply printed money to cover the costs of the sections of the economy that had been forced to close.

The question at the time of writing is what vision of the economy will the government opt for as we move into a post-pandemic world? Will be plunged into another 'new age of austerity',[1] or will they, now that the genie is out of the bottle, adopt a different tone and move towards spending their way out of trouble?

Rather than confront these generation-defining questions head on, this chapter dives deep into the government machine in order to explore the role the civil service plays in the generation of economic myth. The civil service is meant to provide unbiased evidence for the policies the government pursue, and as such, are supposed to help prevent policy from veering too far into the realm of myth. However, the time I spent in Whitehall indicated that, when it comes to the economy, the principal of basing policy on evidence as opposed to evidence on policy is something of a smokescreen.

It is not easy to convince economists, or anyone else working in government, to talk openly about their jobs with a lowly researcher like myself. So, as an attempt to develop some trust, I manged to weasel my way into playing for a football team that primarily consisted of government economists. It was good to get a run around each week, and I believe my selfless commitment and positional discipline to that all important defensive midfield role opened up some doors that would otherwise have been closed.

To find out about my teammates' jobs I took to meeting them and their colleagues at their offices in Whitehall. Before each appointment I would wait in large lobbies full of suited people, who I assumed had been summoned there for important, maybe life changing, meetings with state officials. I'd sit and watch them as they waited nervously, until someone arrived to whisk them away into the bowels of one of the massive bureaucratic office blocks that house our civil service.

In the BIS[2] lobby there is a long reception desk, behind which large TVs play low budget shows about the excellency of the department. When I was there, part of the lobby had been sectioned off for a small exhibition with photos and uplifting stories about start-ups, surrounded by Union Jacks. The magnitude of the building dwarfed this small display that nobody took any notice of.

Once your contact has come to collect you, you are given a pass and enter the building's inner chambers. First you are confronted with a large round hall of pod-like cylindrical lifts. After that (it doesn't matter which floor you arrive on, they are all the same), you are met with a huge open-plan office spreading out from the lift halls in the centre. Many of the meeting rooms in these offices are glass walled. Often, I would be in one of these meeting rooms talking to an economist or policy advisor, while meetings either side of me would be going on. I couldn't hear the other meetings, but it felt as though nothing was separating me from them. It was like a panopticon.

The institution behind the myth

I initially felt slightly uncomfortable when travelling to Whitehall, as there is a palpable change when you move from where I live in North London towards the centre of town. The tube stations you exit from are much grander than the ones you enter into. People are smartly dressed; important meetings about the county's future are taking place; big decisions are being made by important people.

Perhaps to counter my inferiority complex, I read up on the civil service before I began speaking to the people who work there. Flicking through its founding document[3] one passage stood out:

> In many offices ... it is found that the superior docility of young men[4] renders it much easier to make

> valuable public servants of them, than those more advanced in life ... The maintenance of discipline is also easier under such circumstances, and regular habits may be enforced, which it would be difficult to impose for the first time on older men.[5]

The quote eased my anxiety and gave me a sense of what the civil service was set up to do – to serve, in whatever way possible, their masters in government. Indeed, the more 'docile' they are the better.

However, when I started reading about the civil service's contemporary incarnation and talking to civil servants, I learned that, in appearance at least, things have changed. Rather than just following orders and doing whatever they are told, civil servants are now required to be politically neutral and, along with carrying out administrative tasks, a major role of many civil servants is the provision of evidence-based advice. One senior Treasury economist told me:

> The whole point about being a civil servant is that you have to be politically neutral ... as long as I've provided evidence-based advice ... then I'm confident that my advice, whatever they choose, is the best advice they can get.[6]

I learned that the majority of the work done by the civil servants working on economic policies concerns conducting research into possible future scenarios, then relaying this research back to a minister. So, whilst civil servants explicitly work for ministers, a major part of the official role of the civil service is to supply ministers with an objective information base upon which the ministers can act.[7]

In recent years there has been a shift in the amount of people employed in the civil service and in the type of evidence they collect. Spending cuts have seen staff numbers decrease from around 530,000 in 2010 to around 455,000 in 2020.[8] Despite this dramatic drop in the number of civil servants, there was almost a tripling in the amount of economists working within the civil service over a slightly longer period: from 607 in 2001 to roughly 1,500 in 2017.[9] This increase in economists working in government infrastructure has been matched by a longer-term consolidating of power over other government departments by the Treasury[10] (the department seen to be driven most by economic logic), causing a number of writers to note the rising importance of the logic of economics in our political institutions.

However, what does this growth in the importance of economics mean? From one perspective, it would appear to indicate that decisions which were previously made on partisan ideological grounds are now being based on the impartial logic of economics: It's not Left, it's not Right, but it's just about looking at the data and 'following the science'.

Maybe. But as we saw when we peered under the bonnet of the financial world, things that seem to be cold, objective and un-swayed by the frailty of human judgement, are not always as neutral as they appear.

Indeed, the first thing that struck me when I started talking to civil servants was that a clear political agenda lurked behind much of the 'objective' economic evidence they were collating. One policy lead described the economists as providing 'ammunition' for the policies he wanted to put forward. And this description seemed to ring true for most of the people I spoke to.

One economist was moving into a policy team, he told me, because it didn't matter what you came up with as an economist, if it didn't match the policy that was being put forward it would be ignored. Another senior economist explained that a large part of his job was about staying in close contact with the minister's private secretary so that he could understand what the minister wanted and help provide the figures for it. And during one of my interviews with a senior policy figure from the Cabinet Office there was admittance that sometimes the books are cooked and economists are given direct instructions telling them to provide figures to justify policies. He told me this in a slightly convoluted, politician-esque, way:

> There were economists working in each of the [content blocked for anonymity] teams that I was coordinating, so I couldn't say exactly whether they had been told what was going to happen and that they had to give some numbers to justify it, but I know that was true in some cases ... you've got these powerful people at the top who've been given a mandate by a minister to the Cabinet Office to roll out their agenda, so it's mostly in-fighting between the different [content blocked for anonymity] teams who are advocating for their own agenda, and if

the environment becomes like that, you don't want evidence that contradicts your agenda.

Given what I had read about how civil servants, especially economists, are supposed to provide objective evidence for ministers to act on, it was surprising to hear such a candid admittance that sometimes the economists are just told to 'give some numbers' to justify policy. But the more I spoke to people, the more this submission of evidence to policy became a running theme; it was like an open secret.

It wasn't that numbers were just made up and plucked out of thin air, it was more that the numbers which were chosen and the ways of presenting them were highly dependent on the briefs the economists were given. One economist explained it like this:

> It [economics] doesn't drive policy, it justifies policy. Like in an academic essay, you've got the argument and then you Google search it to find the support you want.

Consider the following lengthier passage from a discussion between myself and Andrew, a statistical economic analyst:

> Andrew: So, for example today I had to provide some briefing lines … and they go to Number 10. I write these lines, and you know, it might be factually correct, but without being fair, and presenting the evidence in a fair way.

Me: But that then makes it sound a bit like ... you have your argument and then you collect the evidence around it?

Andrew: Personally I think that's probably true ... People say 'this is my ideology and this is the right thing to do', and there's lots of evidence you can use to point to whatever you like really ... it tends to be that the evidence that comes to the surface fits the policy, not the other way round with the policy based on the evidence.

It was pretty clear that economists in the civil service were not just providing neutral objective evidence for their ministers, but that they were being guided, sometimes openly, to marshal the evidence towards policy positions.

This raises the question: why bother with all these economists and their research? I didn't feel bold enough to ask this question outright, it would have been like asking someone if they were a propagandist, but an answer can be found in the philosopher Eleanora Montuschi's work.[11] She writes about the rise in 'evidence-based approaches to policy making', stating that:

> the language of quantification, which has become the emblem of late-modern society, seems not only to carry with it an 'intimidating sense of objectivity', but also to project a misleading or potentially confusing appearance of objectivity when applied to ''non-scientific' evidence.

It's easy to see the appeal of the 'language of quantification' and objectivity in the political realm. Compromise, negotiation and contestation are central aspects of communication for policy makers and politicians, and if you can couch your argument in objective terms it will stand a stronger chance of defeating positions that may counter it. Furthermore, policies are likely to encounter less public scrutiny if they appear to be based on objective reasoning and presented in the language of economics, which is beyond the reach of many citizens.

So, it appears that the representation of policy as being based on objective evidence, rather than *actually* basing policy on objective economic evidence, is the core of what economics is all about in the civil service. As with the financial sector, representation of economic knowledge as being based on cold hard objective logic seemed to be key, regardless of the foundations of that knowledge.

The myth

In one sense, if ministers can dictate how the economy is represented in the civil service, and also how the economy is presented to the public, then there doesn't seem to be much point in exploring economic myth in the civil service – instead we should go straight to the ministers. On the other hand, because of the civil service's role, it acts as something like a kiln, making solid and durable the wet clay briefings its ministers present it with. And it is only once these briefings have been through the kiln, and are translated into the 'language of quantification', that they become solid enough to be projected out into the world. As such, looking at this process in closer detail allows us to deconstruct the overarching myths behind government communication on the economy.

Technical myth

When I asked the economists and policy workers about the role of economics within their work the words 'balance', 'objective' and 'evidence' were frequently used. This sense of objectivity was also apparent from the manner in which economists are referred to in the civil service: they are known as 'analysts'. In the official jargon on government websites an 'analyst' could refer to anyone conducting research for the state (including a number of social science researchers); however, in practice the everyday use of the word 'analyst' refers to economists.[12] The impression this creates is one of expertise, and a sense that there is a 'thing' there to be analysed. A senior economist explained his role to me:

> I understand technical economic concepts like price competition and supply and demand aspects of the labour market, and I can communicate that to ministers who might not be economically technical or literate. That's a main part of my job, communicating technical economic jargon clearly and sincerely.

He understands himself to be communicating something that is *technical*, and the role he adopts is one of an expert or scientist explaining an aspect of the world to his illiterate superiors. The word *technical* has two main definitions which are related to each other:

> Technical – connected with the practical use of machinery, methods, etc. in science and industry; or
>
> Technical – (usually before noun) connected with the skills needed for a particular job, sport, art, etc.[13]

The first definition relates to the thing itself that is being discussed – in this case, economic concepts: 'technical economic concepts like price competition and supply and demand' – and imbues this thing with a practical and almost mechanical aspect. Consider a typical criticism of a cultural artefact, that it is 'technically competent but lacking in heart', implying that it is well put together but lacking in meaning. This indicates how technical qualities are understood to relate to the objective physical observable aspects of the object under consideration, and it illustrates how these technical qualities are contrasted with 'untechnical' human interpretation. If someone tells you they are a 'technician', you will probably consider them to be a type of engineer capable of manipulating and understanding a 'technical' aspect of the physical world.[14] The antithesis of a professional 'technician' would be a professional theorist: one works with matter and the other with ideas. The fact that, in everyday talk, this economist thinks of himself as a technician (and not a theorist) implies that the thing he is working on, 'the economy', is something he understands as having an ontological stability or existence of its own. The manner in which the economy is conceived of and defined here implies the full extent of its abstraction: not only does it take on an existence of its own, but that existence is analogised as being akin to a mechanical and physical entity.

The manner in which he says he 'understands' this thing (the economy) further abstracts it by providing it with its own ontological presence as something to understand. But it also relates to the second definition of 'technical', which is brought out in the notion of someone being 'technically literate', as it implies the expertise or skills needed for someone to understand this 'thing'. Given that in this vision the economy is a technical thing, one also needs technical skills to understand it. These skills come in the currency of economic knowledge, which takes the form of a neutralised discourse on existing phenomena. Consider the following from the same conversation:

> I wouldn't describe myself as an ideological person, I'm much more of a practical person, I'm interested in what works, not some ideology. And economics is a very practical way of looking at the world.

Both civil servants and ministers want to avoid appearing to base decisions on overtly political or ideological justifications. So, regarding economic knowledge as a neutral extrapolation of information from a technical and tangible thing (i.e. the economy) helps them to serve the purposes they see themselves fulfilling, and this contributes to the reification of the economy as an autonomous technical thing that exists out there in the world.

The autonomous economy: morality versus growth (culture versus nature)

'Growth' was frequently used as a property of the economy by the civil servants I spoke to; this choice of word, like the 'technical' discussion above, further reifies the conception of the economy by helping to provide it with an autonomous form. Growth indicates something that can physically expand, but it also has natural connotations, implying that the thing to which the word is applied can grow of its own accord. Everyday statements such as 'the economy has grown by 3% in the last quarter' contain hidden assumptions concerning the type of thing the economy is.[15] However, whilst the use of natural metaphors is not unique to the civil service, the manner in which the civil servants understood economic growth as being something opposed to other aspects of society indicates a potential way in which the economy is defined against other phenomena.

Economic growth by creating a 'competitive' but 'fair' economy was the underlying goal that all my interviewees wished to achieve through their work. 'Flexibility/competitiveness' represents the free market, the ability of businesses to hire, fire and trade, unimpinged by laws protecting workers and consumers (i.e. it leads to growth); and 'fairness' refers to the rights of workers and consumers not to be exploited (i.e. it ensures morality). This compromise, between morality and growth, is the central ethic that runs through the vision of the economy in the civil service.

The consistent proliferation of the notion of 'economic issues' as something opposed to more moral issues, such as 'workers' rights', illuminates something beyond just seeing the economy as autonomous from other societal aspects, as it provides the economy with a logical and (im)moral force. At the time of writing, during the COVID-19 crisis, this is abundantly apparent in the manner in which the economy is being pitted against public health. A dualism is created between 'economic logic' on one side and 'moral logic' on the other. The economy becomes a detached sphere of its own, with a logical force of its own – furthermore, a sphere and logic that is opposed to moral aspects of society.

However, when pushed, the view most of the civil servants subscribed to was that 'the economy' is a balancing force, as it harnesses aspects of human nature whilst also protecting society when those aspects overflow and become harmful. From this perspective, the economy is a combination of nature and culture, an essentialised force and the civilised reaction to it, which harnesses nature but at the same time restricts it. This came out most strikingly in a conversation I had with a policy advisor in the Treasury. We were discussing how he understood the economy, and the conversation had taken a philosophical turn:

> So, in the broadest terms our economic system is capitalist, and I think people are fundamentally

> self-interested. So, capitalism works in the way that it incentivises, and I think that capitalism has been the most successful economic system that we've ever seen, and in some ways that implies that it fits with human nature, just through that kind of pragmatic experience of it working so ... yeah, I guess I'd say in real terms that our economy works in such a way that it incentivises in line with human nature.

He went on:

> I think the economy needs to balance human nature, because the strongest people in society will always want to strengthen their position. So, you need a strong welfare state, you need minimum wage and that sort of thing, just fundamental things to ensure that equality exists, or a degree of equality or equal opportunity exists within society; I think there's always going to be a tendency for self-interest, thus you always have to protect the interests of everyone in society, and that would be my fundamental stance on it.

A central aspect of the vision is the notion of an innate essentialised drive: 'human nature', which needs to be balanced by moral considerations to try and ensure equality. If we further deconstruct this notion of the economy, it is possible to understand that the moral aspects of the economy exist only in relation to the more foundational notion of competitive human nature at the base of the concept. The other aspects of the economy, the cultural or moral aspects like the welfare state or workers' rights, are brought into existence only as a reaction to the base drive (i.e. to protect us from it). As the quote above testifies, in this economic vision, the current economic settlement is successful because it has not strayed too far from these innate drives[16].

Whilst, in the broad philosophical perspective outlined above, selfish human nature and morality were both seen to be part of 'the economy', in the everyday language used when people weren't consciously trying to define it for me, the economy was presented in a different moral light to other issues. Consider the quote below from a policy worker:

> if the law's not quite working I have to find ways to change the law that strikes a balance for employees' rights and doesn't cause unnecessary problems for employers ... if we have too stringent employment laws it could hinder growth for businesses or the way they could operate in the labour market, which is damaging to the economy because we need the UK economy to prosper ... the conservative side of the government are more aligned to the employer / the business, to make sure the business can operate and that is very driven by the economic challenges for the country. And the Lib Dems and the Labour Party are very much aligned to employees' rights and not exploiting workers.

We see here again, how 'the economy' (i.e. growth) is defined in distinction to other moral aspects of society (i.e. not exploiting workers). So there seems to be a difference between the 'official' philosophical view that the people I spoke to adhere to (which is demonstrated above through my conversation with the policy lead in the Treasury) and the way the economy is defined in the everyday language used in the civil service. In the broader philosophical vision, the economy consists of both innate human nature and moral cultural institutions (although the human-nature aspect appeared to be more fundamental). However, in everyday discourse the economy is defined in distinction to moral cultural institutions.

A vision of the economy that separates it out from other cultural aspects of society helps promote the myth of the economy as an autonomous entity. On one side you have the human aspects of morality and kindness, which are represented by the welfare state and workers' rights, and on the other side you have a detached sphere driven by the need to grow, and based on the cold hard facts of human nature.

As argued in the previous chapter, reifying the economy as a detached impersonal sphere helps facilitate the pot of money myth. When, in the 1980s, Margaret Thatcher wrought the most dramatic economic reforms the UK had seen in generations she used the slogan 'There is no alternative'. This slogan encapsulates the way in which reifying the economy as an autonomous entity can be weaponised for political ends. She was saying we must obey the economy, as we are simply powerless in the face of it! In this vision, agency moves from our hands (as represented by the elected government) to the hands of a reified autonomous thing called *the economy*.

When the Chancellor, Rishi Sunak, talks about the 'hard choices' we face in light of the COVID-19 deficit and that he has a 'sacred responsibility'[17] to balance the books, he is drawing on the same vision of the economy as something separate from us that we must obey. When he tells us that we will need to pay all the money back and that there are only two ways to fill the pot back up again (through tax and borrowing),[18] he is lying to us, and doing it through the guise of the of the pot of money myth.

He is ignoring the other option, that the government can and does print vast sums of money through the Bank of England (as discussed later in the book), yet this fact is ignored as it does not fit into the simple vision of the economy as a pot of money that he wants to present to the public. Instead, just as Thatcher did before him and as the entire austerity narrative does, he is fuelling the myth that the nation's economy is something akin to a household budget. And the conceptual separation of the economy from other human endeavours that is present in the civil service facilitates this mythological framing.

Moving now from the macro to the micro, by taking a close-up look at the setting of an economic policy, we can see how the reification of the economy, and economic knowledge as an objective neutral discourse, is not only weaponised in how the economy is mythologised by the government, but also in the setting of individual policies.

Case study: economics in policy

The National Minimum Wage (NMW) was – and under its current guise as the National Living Wage is – the minimum hourly rate for every employee in the UK. It was introduced as a controversial element of Tony Blair's 1997 electoral manifesto, as a former NMW Commissioner explains:

> The National Minimum Wage was the ugly duckling of the 1997 Labour Government. The proposal had been a favourite target of Conservative attack during the election campaign, with blood-chilling predictions of its unemployment implications. The Labour leadership's response had been nervously defensive. The commitment to a statutory minimum wage had been forced on them by Party Conference and it threatened to undermine their prime objectives of winning business confidence and reducing unemployment.[19]

In 1996 David Cameron, then a prospective MP for Stratford, announced that the NMW 'would send unemployment straight back up',[20] with some economists predicting that unemployment would increase by 2 million following its initial introduction.[21] This didn't happen, and there is no evidence to show that introducing the NMW, or the subsequent changes to it, affected unemployment. A few years after its introduction, all major political parties in the UK supported the NMW.

It went from being an extremely controversial policy to what many have considered the best legacy of Blair's premiership, winning a prize from *The Political Studies Association* for the most successful government policy in the last 30 years. Indeed, in July 2015 it was increased significantly by Cameron's conservative government.

Prior to the change in 2015 this tension between different perspectives on the NMW played out while it was being negotiated each year by a group set up by the government called the Low Pay Commission (LPC).

The rate was re-evaluated and set on a yearly basis through a process of negotiation between nine Low Pay Commissioners: three represented workers (senior trades union figures); three represented businesses (Confederation of British Industries representatives and senior figures in the businesses world); and three were academic economists. As one former Commissioner explained to me: 'the remit was to benefit the lowest paid by pushing the NMW as high as we possibly can without any direct impact on employment or wider economic matters'.

The LPC's mission was a classic morality vs growth scenario: they were to prevent exploitation of workers by pushing wages up as much as possible without negatively impacting businesses. This framing illustrates sympathy with economic orthodoxy through the notion that higher wages will force businesses to let workers go and that the ideal scenario would be a market equilibrium in which labour supply and demand coincided according to market principals, as wages above the market equilibrium would cause unemployment. But, due to various factors, the free-market equilibrium is not reached 'naturally' and workers get exploited, so the free-market equilibrium position needs to be coaxed into position. In summary, the LPC were presented as helping the market do its job, rather than acting against it.

In seeking out this equilibrium the LPC strived for a compromise between the different demands its members were put under by the employees and employers they represented. The negotiations they undertook each year were based on understanding the 'economic evidence' presented to them, and applying it to economic models in order to make future predictions. As such, looking at the NMW and its 2015 metamorphosis into the National Living Wage provides us with an excellent case study for the relationship between economics and policy, as it would be hard to find a more ostensibly objective, evidence-based economic policy.[22]

Unlike most other civil servants, and those discussed previously in this chapter, the LPC's secretariat who were tasked with collecting the economic evidence did not respond directly to a minister and in order to avoid political contamination were housed in a different building to their colleagues. All the members of the secretariat I spoke to insisted that it was the most objective evidence-based team they had been part of. However, despite this, I discovered a degree of cynicism regarding 'the evidence', as one of the secretariat explained:

> We were a small organisation and the chief economist had a crucial role and had a lot of influence over the interpretation and the commissioning of

> evidence. So, I think an individual in that position can have as much influence as a minister might in terms of their views of what the world looks like, and having some influence on how the evidence is interpreted and what evidence is followed or not followed.

The implication here is that even without having to respond to a minister there are decisions to be made about the collection of evidence and how the evidence is interpreted and then operationalised. Consider the following quotation from an economist in the secretariat concerning why the NMW was significantly lower for those under the age of 21:

> economists are, not like cults exactly, but like religions, and they sit in certain areas and they hold certain world views, and it's quite interesting how rigidly people stick to those ... for example we have youth rates and we have a consultation every year with different organisations. And the National Union of Students are very critical of the youth rates, as a number of youth groups are. They say they're unfair and they say there's no evidence that young people are less productive and that this is just bias and prejudices against young people. So ... our chief economist will just say; 'this is absolute nonsense!' And he'll probably attribute it to the fact that in countries where there's just one minimum wage, there's very high youth unemployment. And he will also say, 'well clearly they're less productive because they don't have the skills

> and the experience'. So that's something he'll stick to rigidly ... but coming at it from a completely different position you think well, why is this so accepted? And you realise it's a case where ideology is determining how the data is treated.

Here we see a case in which different economists disagree over the meaning of the same data, but the decision as to how the data is interpreted lies with the chief economist. So again, we see how a top-down institutionalised hierarchal chain influences the type of knowledge that is produced. Furthermore, the presentation of this knowledge had a very real effect on the economic organisation of British society – in this case the NMW for people under the age of 21 remained significantly lower than for those over 21.

However, aside from the 'tribes' that certain economists belong to and the institutional pressure for researchers to present evidence in a manner that fits with their superiors' 'worldview', there is a broader question concerning why certain types of knowledge prevail over others. Oren Levin-Waldman, a political economist in the US, has written extensively about the minimum wage. He explains how institutional norms account for why some visions triumph over others:

> the starting point of the orthodoxy is the goal of efficiency; the minimum wage can only be beneficial public policy to the extent that it can be shown that the benefits outweigh the costs. Competing visions, by contrast, begin with the starting point

> of what type of society we would like to achieve and how the minimum wage can be employed in the service of that vision.[23]

Levin-Waldman's quote demonstrates how one vison of 'economic' logic (efficiency) is privileged over social logic in the way the policy question is framed, and how this determines the outcome. A former Commissioner told me how this functioned in the setting of the British minimum wage:

> The Low Pay Commission, by its very nature, and by the remit, is intrinsically conservative, because you're saying put wages up but without any adverse economic indicators (and) you can always find an adverse economic indicator.

A member of the secretariat explained further:

> If you removed the requirement to take account of unemployment ... then it may be easier for the Commissioners to say 'well let's take a chance on higher wages'.

As this quote shows, the manner in which the question is framed in the remit shapes the conclusion reached. The requirement that it should take account of unemployment framed the setting of the NMW in a particular way and allows for it to be measured according to economic principals. As a data analyst told me:

> The way that the objective is set out, is that, in order to maximise the minimum wage subject to

not having a detrimental impact on employment, gives us a way of measuring it.

As already noted, prior to the initial setting of the NMW in 1999 there were a number of economists whose 'objective' models made them certain that the introduction of the NMW would immediately result in millions of people losing their jobs (it didn't). In the case of the LPC, the remit situated the decision of where to set the NMW within a model that provided a conservative approach to increases, and allowed those who wished to keep it low an 'objective' logic to do so.

During the LPC's negotiation, which is between two polarised factions (trades unions and the business community), all the Commissioners I spoke to emphasised that it was only the shared mission of pushing up the NMW without affecting employment, combined with a respect for economic evidence, that allowed a compromise to be reached. Yet, as shown above, the 'objective' economic logic favoured those with a desire to keep the NMW low, indicating that it might not be so 'objective' after all.

Changes to the NMW

When announcing the 'emergency budget' in July 2015, the Chancellor, George Osborne, declared that 'Britain deserves a pay rise' and promised to increase the NMW to £9 by 2020 (as I write in 2021 it's £8.72). To put this into context, under the LPC the adult NMW increased from £6.08 in 2011 to £6.50 in 2015, increases of around 3%

each year. Following the 2015 change it has increased at roughly 6% each year. Furthermore, the rhetoric around the NMW and how it is calculated was significantly re-arranged. It became known as the 'National Living Wage' and, rather than through a compromise reached by the LPC, it is set at 60% of the median hourly earnings.[24]

This change in policy effectively made the LPC's role redundant in setting the adult NMW, as Osborne was telling them what they will recommend, thus rendering any pretence of political objectivity farcical.

What does it mean, then, to say that economic policy is based on political rather than 'objective economic' rationale? In this case it's possible to analyse some of what could be called the political motivations for the policy. There appear to be two overt reasons Osborne and his party set to benefit from the 2015 change in the NMW: firstly, it stole the thunder from their main political rivals, as they were adopting one of Labour's most popular policies; secondly, it grabbed the headlines and provided a counterbalance to austerity, which Osborne used in order to justify the implementation of economic policies more in line with the traditional ethos of his party. As well as announcing a dramatic increase in a universally popular policy (the NMW), Osborne's budget also contained a number of welfare cuts, aimed at slimming down state spending.

As a result of these changes, the Institute for Fiscal Studies (hardly a bastion of left-wing interventionist policy)[25] produced the following chart (see Figure 2 overleaf), which illustrates who benefited from the budget and who didn't:

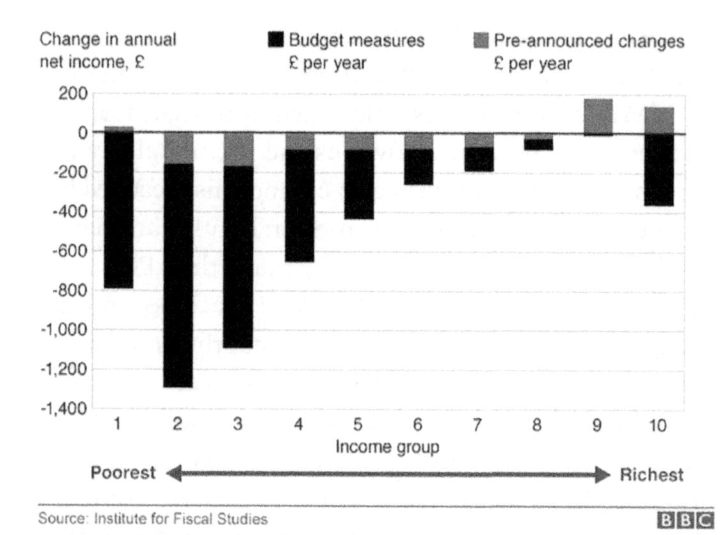

Figure 2 Impact of tax and benefit reforms, 2015–2019
Source: based on B. Milligan, 'Budget 2015: Squeeze to Hit 13m Families, says IFS' (9 July 2015), BBC, www.bbc.co.uk/news/business-33463864 (accessed 31 March 2021). Data taken from the IFS, which can be found in A. Bourqin, A. Norris Keiller and T. Waters, *The Distributional Impact of Personal Tax and Benefit Reforms, 2010–2019* (2019), www.ifs.org.uk/publications/14597 (accessed 31 March 2021).

Seen in this context, it's clear that the rise in the NMW was supposed to compensate for the reduction in tax credits that the poorer members of society were dealt, but as Figure 2 indicates, it came nowhere near to compensating for the cuts. The NMW is well suited to being a Trojan horse in this manner since it is easy for the public and media to understand compared to other economic policies, and raising it will almost always be popular with the electorate.

When the NMW was being set by the LPC it stood as good a chance as any economic policy of being based on unbiased objective economic evidence; it had a highly skilled independent secretariat presenting evidence to two evenly matched teams, each supporting opposing perspectives, with three expert economists making sure that the arguments constructed by each team corroborated with the evidence. However, the framing of the question provided those with a desire to keep it low a rationale to do so. And this framing made what was ostensibly a political decision (as how the question was framed was determined by the government, and the framing determined the outcome) appear to be a politically neutral choice based on objective economic logic.

Lessons

Meddling with the minimum wage pales into insignificance with the changes in economic policy the political class are now faced with. We are in the midst of a health crisis that, at the time of writing, has cost the government around £340 billion.[26] Whole industries are facing annihilation as the government are paying the wages of 8 million furloughed workers, yet how these debts will be serviced and whether or not the government will continue supporting the private sector are unclear. On top of this, there is the question of Brexit: new laws, policies and trade deals will need to come into effect as the UK emerges from its relationship with the EU, and seeks to forge a new economy.

What this chapter has shown is that, if we want to be able to understand and evaluate the economic policies our government is pursuing, we cannot leave it up to them to inform us. Ministers will hide behind the 'language of quantification' when they present us with the policies that shape our world.

Aside from the urgency of questioning economic policy, some light has also been shone on the sense of disconnect, mistrust and anger many people feel towards political elites. The people whom I spoke to on the estate would not be at all surprised to learn that economic discourse in the political sphere is so charged with bias that it often deliberately misrepresents reality. They have given up hope of trusting mainstream politicians, and seeing the extent of political opportunism in the government's economic discourse, it's easy to understand why.

Furthermore, not only do the economic narratives in the political sphere misrepresent reality, they also feed into a myth of the economy as an autonomous entity, and present growth as its fundamental characteristic. In this myth there is a trade-off between a happy (growing) economy and the culturally imposed moral restrictions of the welfare state. Therefore, according to this logic, to keep the economy growing we must rein in the restrictions the state place on it, as this will unleash its natural productive forces.

What this means in practice is a prioritisation of the productivity of firms, at the cost of other more ethical goals that a broader conception of the economy might encompass. And this brings into focus another myth that is at the heart of our economic system – the notion that our societies must be organised in a way that leads to maximum production. That this myth persists in the face of the environmental crisis is alarming, as now more than ever, we need to reassess the drive to produce more more more.

Yet, even if we ignore global warming and accept that productivity is the key to a happy economy, the idea that the best way to achieve this is to rein in the state and let 'the economy' *do its thing*, is riven with contradictions. Austerity was based on the notion that we could fill the pot back up through cutting back on welfare spending and on state intervention in order to make a leaner more competitive and more productive economy. But looking at the evidence more than a decade after the policy was introduced, we can see an unprecedented drop in productivity (20%) – worse than any comparable nation. On top of this, real wages (i.e. adjusting for inflation) have stood still since 2008, which is also almost unprecedented in the modern era.[27]

So, not only does the myth generated by the political sphere create and disseminate a vision of the economy that is divorced from reality, it has helped lead to a situation in which we are producing less and being paid less. While at the same time, the basic services many rely on for a dignified existence have been sacrificed like lambs at 'the economies' alter.

If we can't trust the government or financiers to tell us about the economy, the last bastion of shining hope falls on the shoulders of our next site of exploration; the UK's free and robust media.

4
Media myths

If finance and politics both disseminate a myth of the economy that feeds into the notion of it as something akin to a pot of money, then the only place that could challenge this elite vision is the media. Indeed, one of the key roles the media is meant to play in modern democracies is to act as a counterbalance to the elite powers explored in the previous two chapters (big business and the state).

In democratic theory there are three overlapping roles the media is supposed to play: 1) to inform the public about the world around them; 2) to act as a 'watchdog' highlighting any negative behaviour that the public should be aware of; and 3) to act as a space for public deliberation, which can inform decision makers about what the public desires and apply pressure on them to deliver it. So, in an ideal democracy, the media will be a source of public information, keep elites in check, and act as something like a go-between for elite decision makers and the broader population.

When it comes to the economy, this democratic role takes on extra significance. The economy is, let's face it, complicated. So, the media's role as a purveyor of information is key: we need economic journalism to help us understand our economy, assess the economic decisions our leaders make, and expose anything untoward in the worlds of business and politics.

However, the post-2008 recession and the rise of the internet have accelerated a longer-term crisis in the news-production business model. The newsroom workforce in US newspapers has shrunk by around 50% over the past decade[1] and in the UK, national newspapers are losing sales at a rate of 10% year on year.[2] The same grim outlook applies to television and online news,[3] which now has to compete with social media and entertainment providers like Netflix. The impact of this difficult business context has resulted in major cutbacks to news-gathering budgets, and a decline in the quality and quantity of serious journalism.

Economic coverage has been one of the casualties. Reporting on the economy requires greater time to be taken, by the reporter investigating the story and also by the audience member, as both will need to engage with complex material. As such, economic reportage does not lend itself to the high-speed way we produce and consume news in the twenty-first century.

The result of this difficult business context has been a polarisation of different types of economic reporting. On the one hand, there is abundant detailed coverage of economic issues in media outlets like Bloomberg or in *The Financial Times*, aimed at those who have a specific interest in the financial markets (i.e. people with enough money to invest). On the other hand, the coverage in these specialist publications is inaccessible, incomprehensible and often irrelevant to the vast majority of the population, leaving scant serious economic reportage in the news media that most people engage with.

In what follows I outline the time I spent nosing about at the offices of one of the UK's leading financial magazines. I selected the magazine as, while it is a specialist publication, it is also advertised as bridging the gap between expert investors and the person on the street. As such, I thought it would be a suitable space to explore the generation and dissemination of economic myth in the media.

The institutional context behind the myth

Selling the economy

The *Money Matters*[4] office was located on the eighth floor of an imposing office block in central London. The office was open-plan and the magazine's staff shared the space with the people who worked on other products produced by the magazine's parent company. During my time there, I never saw the office more than three-quarters full; this was because working from home was accepted by the company, and many of the staff members worked part-time.

The print copy of the magazine had a circulation of around 50,000 (one of the biggest financial magazines in the UK), and there were also daily emails with investment advice and punchy articles about the financial news, which were sent out for free to around 100,000 people. These emails advertised the magazine and marketed the other products that the company sold.

The magazine had only started to make a profit in the last couple of years. Its main role within the marketing model of the organisation was to interest customers by appealing to the general public, who could then be funnelled through to the financial newsletters which were sent to subscribers via email and contained investment advice combined with an entertaining and opinionated narrative. The newsletters generated greater profit than the magazine, so the company tried eventually to move customers onto the more expensive newsletters, which could cost up to £500 per year. One of the editors explained:

> Marketing is an integral part of this company … it's sort of the whole operation, from the magazine to the newsletters to the back-end newsletters, it's all one big operation. It's all for the same type of people, we try and filter people through; the magazine might reach a very large number of people but we will try and pull the most interested people all the way through and reap as much money as we can off them.

The model is about trying to build relationships with as many people as possible and then trying to drag them through from the cheap 'front-end' products (the free emails written by copywriters and the magazine) to the more expensive 'back-end' products (the newsletters written by specialists), from which the company generates most of its profit. Lyudmila, one of the company's marketing executives, elaborated on how this business model helps shape the representation of the economy in the magazine and newsletters:

> Lyudmila: Our ideas for marketing come from the editorial but we have to frame them in a way that's going to make people subscribe.
>
> Me: Which you do by being simple and clear?
>
> Lyudmila: Yeah, simple and clear and by telling people: 'you need this or you will die!' Hahaha.
>
> Me: Fear and greed?
>
> Lyudmila: Greed and fear, I find fear mostly works with *Money Matters*, tell people the world is coming to an end and they have to subscribe to do something about it.
>
> Me: But I suppose that's more with the newsletters than with the magazine?
>
> Lyudmila: Even with *Money Matters* we've found that most of our promotions have been very fear-led, saying, you know, you have to dump these toxic investments because you're going to go down … it works really well … but also we genuinely believe that is going to happen; we don't just make it up to try and scare people.

Whilst Lyudmila said 'we don't just make it up to try and scare people', there does seem to be a clear pressure to tell a certain kind of story. This need to emphasise the economy as something that can destroy you or make you wealthy was central to what many other employees told me about the company's approach to writing and, as we will see later, it helps facilitate a certain vison of the economy.

Further to the need for it to appeal to fear and greed I was informed that the writing also had to be entertaining, as one of the co-founders put it:

> Actually we are, in the end, all of us, in show business. And let's not pretend otherwise ... in the end we're there to sell copies of this magazine and therefore it has to be, if nothing else, entertaining, so it has to be made fun; if it's dull no one will buy it.

These quotes illustrate clear examples of themes that ran through the conversations I had at *Money Matters*. The presentation of economic knowledge in an entertaining and simplified form, along with the pressure to provoke emotional responses in the readers through 'fear and greed', was central to how staff talked about their writing.

As the motives shift from the democratic ideals outlined at the start of the chapter, towards the company's profit margin, it's easy to see the distancing of the discourse from solid empirical evidence or thorough epistemological grounding, as it moves into symbolic and emotive registrars. As will be argued later, these pressures have the effect of emphasising the myth of the economy as an autonomous organic entity. However, before we get to that, let's look at some other pressures that shape the representation of the economy in the media.

Sounding like an expert

Money Matters was set up in the late 1990s by a former trader and a well-established current-affairs journalist as a digest of the weekly financial news. Noting how more individuals were investing their money in stocks and shares – as a consequence of the tech bubble of the 1990s, the general rise in household incomes and the widespread use of the internet – the magazine's co-founders thought they saw a gap in the market for a magazine that would digest the financial news in an entertaining fashion, easily understood by the lay-person. However, the magazine was initially unsuccessful and failed to generate profit until it changed its style and became opinion-led rather than digest-led. One of the co-founders explained to me:

> if you look at the early editions of the magazine you will see that there was nothing original in it, there was no opinion, it was purely a digest of interesting stuff that we had read. What happened was it didn't sell very well; it sold a bit but not very well. And it gradually became clear to us that there was a difference between the way you could sell current affairs and the way you could sell money information. In that ... digest works perfectly well in current affairs because people have a view in current affairs already ... they already know where they stand on the spectrum, they have information, all you need to do is to provide them with the information on a particular subject and they know their own opinion ... But with money

> it's very different, because no one really has a view on where the yield on Danish sovereign debt is going to go. They don't have that already because there is no view to take. So, offering them a digest where you say 'well so and so says this, and so and so says that, now go and make up your own minds' is the worst thing you can possibly do, because it simply gives people more information which they are unable to use. So, the turning point for the magazine was saying: OK, so and so says the gold price is going to rise, so and so says the gold prices is going to fall, and I am telling you that the second person is an idiot and the gold price is going to rise, so you need to go out and buy some gold, and this is how I think you should do it ... It was that shift to being very firmly opinionated and offering a very powerful view.

This emphasis on how the magazine needed to be opinionated in order to sell well was also shared by the other co-founder, who summarised it differently:

> In a way, that thing about an ounce of passion is worth a ton of fact is relevant here. You can get things wrong, but if you take a pretty strong view, people like that.

When taking on new staff and training them, the need to be opinionated and convincing was also prominent, as the chief newsletter editor explained:

> Whenever a new editor comes in, the first thing I say to them is, and the first thing that was said to

> me was, 'you have to imagine yourself talking to the smartest person that you know and you need to convince them that they need to do something urgent to change their life because there's a great ominous risk approaching'.

It's possible to see how this need to take strong opinions could come at the cost of thorough grounded analysis, as in this business 'an ounce of passion is worth a ton of fact'. Echoing the conversations I had with people working in the City of London, one of the senior magazine writers, who had previously worked in the City, elaborated on how this need to be opinionated cuts across the financial world:

> The thing that I've learned about finance is that there are no right answers ... yet the way that people comment about finance suggests that there is. This is an industry which is full of very forthright people who have strong opinions and who defend them to the hilt.

What the boss says goes

Whilst all the journalists I spoke to were very clear about the need to take a strong opinion, they were less clear about what their opinions were based on. Many of them had trained as journalists and found themselves drawn to writing about the economy because it was more lucrative than working in other fields of journalism. They often had little or no previous training in finance or economics, and were therefore susceptible to accepting the 'company line', as it provided them with a readymade platform upon which to base their strong opinions. At *Money Matters* I found that senior members of staff tended to have stronger opinions about the underlying forces behind the economy than their junior counterparts. These opinions often rested on notions about the free market being an expression of competitive human nature.[5] The chief newsletter editor gave me a lively account of his view of humankind:

> It's like we're this small aggressive bandit species that grew up in a hunter-gatherer environment, and that is incapable of understanding the complexity of the society that we live in.

The closer the fit between an individual journalist's personal ethos and the wider ethos of the company, the more likely the journalist is to succeed within the company; the institutional hierarchy was therefore mirrored by a kind of hierarchy of strong opinions on the economy. This analysis could be extended all the way up to the owner, who contributes to the magazine with his own weekly column. While he could only be seen in the office once every couple of months, the owner's presence could always be felt, with his name coming up in all the conversations I had with staff members. I was told that he was an extremely wealthy foreign 'stocks and shares guru' with strong libertarian principals, who had purchased the magazine because he was an Anglophile and desired to own a quaint English publication, and chose this particular magazine because his libertarian views chimed with those of the magazine's editor.

Indeed, when I asked one of the senior writers, who had been at the magazine for a while. if he'd seen much change, he responded:

> The personnel has changed and the office has changed but I don't think the ethos has changed, because it's been the same people running it. Sammy Saunders [the owner] ... He basically is the heart and soul of *Money Matters* ... And I think that while somebody like Sammy is controlling it, it isn't going to change.
>
> Sammy's the guy that broadly sets the tone but the actual editorial direction's been set by Clair and Henry [the chief editors] and that's been pretty consistent. They've kept to pretty much the same sort of story.

But some of the junior writers expressed more cynicism towards the 'company line'. As one of them told me:

> I think reporters just have to take on company lines; it's just something you have to accept, you need a paid job at the end of the day. As much as you'd like to be writing about independent stuff you need a job to run your house and all the rest of it.

Consider the following slightly awkward exchange between me and one of the newer members of the writing team:

> Alex: This company has a very particular editorial line that's been like, informed by their view of theory.

Me: What is the theory?

Alex: It's Austrian, roughly, you know, you just tweak some assumptions at the bottom and you end up with a completely different set of views on how the world should work. That's the *Money Matters* staple and I guess most of our writers lean that way.

Me: So when you're spitballing ideas, you always know kind of what the senior editors want and they're always going to be vaguely in line with that?

Alex: Yep, but I think pretty much everybody fits into the same school.

Me: That's interesting. Do you subscribe to that school?

Alex: No not really, errm, not really no.

Me: But I guess you're just doing your job?

Alex: You can't like. Errm I'm not sure. But yeah like. Errm … you're not really seeking truth in journalism all the time, you … I'm new to it I shouldn't be so cynical but I … I think you definitely want to know your audience's erogenous zones and you want to work them. I mean … I wouldn't be so conceited as to think that I write what I believe.

As indicated by the above quotes, journalists who most strongly espouse the company's ethos are the ones who stay at the company and end up becoming senior staff members, so the survival of the 'company line' is assured. We can see here how the institutional arrangement of the company lends a self-perpetuating aspect to the discourse that is being produced.

This issue isn't unique to *Money Matters*. Just three companies dominate 90% of the national newspaper market, while if we include online content, 80% of the market is dominated by the same three companies.[6] Media scholars are increasingly concerned about the ability of a few individuals at the top of these organisations to set agendas.

When it comes to economic journalism this critique takes on extra significance, as the wealthy owners of publications have an interest in maintaining the economic status quo, and perpetuating a free-market ideology, lest the government seek to infringe on their profit-making activity. The media scholar Anu Kantola's thoroughly researched work on *The Financial Times* and other major economic publications has shown how a free-market ideology consistently dominates the financial press, and is even placed above democratic principles.[7] It's hard not to link this ideological leaning to the interests of the owners of outlets that espouse it.

An exclusive community

In keeping with the need to conform to the 'company line', there were a number of other pressures that helped homogenise the discourse produced at *Money Matters*. Research into writing an article was primarily based on information taken from other media outlets, and all the journalists told me that they mainly took their lead from big multinational media organisations such as Bloomberg and Reuters or from *The Financial Times*. The immediacy of the internet allows journalists to conduct their research from their desks; in this instance, one of its effects appeared to be the production of a more homogeneous discourse, as it encouraged different journalists to draw from the same stocks of information.

Furthermore, the magazine and the newsletters are ultimately bound up in the processes of investment capitalism. They are for people with enough money to invest and, as such, they form part of the investment process by informing potential investors where they should or should not put their money. They are then part of the system that they pass comment on, and part of a world which is beyond the capability of most people to enter into. The work of media and communications scholar, Damian Tambini, stresses this point. Through his interviews with financial journalists and editors he notes that the idea that their job had something to do with serving the public was not one that registered:

> For those journalists that aspire to 'public interest' coverage, just what interest should they serve is a very complex issue: should they serve investors? Or the 'rationality' of the market? Only exceptional individuals will actively want to be the one that burst the bubble.[8]

To consider the discourse produced at *Money Matters* from this perspective brings in the notion of broader structural power relations, indicating that the discourse, and the vision of the economy that it promotes, serve the interests of one section of society, rather than fulfilling its democratic role.

Events, my dear boy, events

Before concluding this section on the institution behind the myth, there is one issue I want to touch on, as it is noted in almost all the studies that look at the economy in the media: economic coverage faces a critical problem in its role as an educator because the focus is always on events rather than the broader structure of the economy.

As discussed above, the majority of discourse on the economy in the media is aimed at the investing class. In this coverage there is little incentive for journalists to write about how the economy functions; it is assumed that the reader will already have sufficient background knowledge. Besides, these readers aren't interested in lengthy discussions about different economic systems. Readers of this type of economic journalism want to be 'told where the yield of Danish sovereign debt is going' or whether they should buy or sell gold. The focus of this type of reportage is on specificities of this kind and how they will impact the reader, not on elucidating and questioning how the overall economy functions.

When economic stories make it into the mainstream press, it is usually due to there being some kind of cataclysmic event that just can't be kept off the front pages. The 2008 financial crisis and its aftermath is a case in point. If we go back to a younger version of myself, pacing my parents' living room with BBC News 24 on and trying to make sense of it, then it's possible to see the difficulty economic journalists face in trying to communicate with an economically illiterate public. In order to engage with what I was watching unfold on the news channels, I would have needed a substantial amount of background information about the structure of the global economy.

I could feel the immediacy and importance of what was happening, but I did not understand it. Mainstream economic coverage competes for airtime with far more engaging news items and other forms of entertainment. In a world where concentration spans are becoming shorter and shorter, news media stands little chance of engaging disinterested members of the public in discussions around the different economic systems available to us, or indeed in how our economic system actually functions. Instead, it describes events as they unfold, without exploring how they arose.[9]

If we borrow from the nature metaphors, which, as discussed below, are often found in economic reportage, we can see these events are like the froth of waves on a deep ocean: the broader economic structure is ignored while the surface elements make up the media coverage. The effect of this is that media coverage of the economy fails to perform one of its critical democratic functions – it fails to educate the public about how our economy works.

Myth in the media

What type of myth do these pressures on economic discourse in the media give rise to? Of course, any complex and abstract phenomenon like the economy will always be couched in language that is heavy in metaphor, and therefore will always be reified in one manner or another. But how something is reified matters, as it has implications for how we interpret the world and, therefore, how we act.

The economy as an autonomous natural entity

A number of authors have recorded the manner in which metaphors in the media reify the economy as a living organism.[10] Their analysis shows how media discourse creates a visceral conception of the economy as something akin to an autonomous creature, a force whose power we must harness rather than attempt to tame. One of the senior writers encapsulated this vision of the economy when he explained to me:

> It's this beast that we are incapable of understanding, and it also works because of that. It functions as this thing that is apart from us, it's not meant to be centrally controlled, it's this amorphous thing that keeps evolving.

This vision was also present in the pages of the magazine. Consider the following everyday example of economic discourse in the press:

> This week markets forgot about Greece and concentrated on Spain, which appears to be imploding. It looks set to be overwhelmed by the cost of shoring up its banks, especially as it has no chance of returning to growth anytime soon.

The quotation above reifies economic phenomena in two ways: firstly, it assumes that the 'markets' and the Spanish economy are bounded and objectivised things with realities of their own. This objectification is exemplified by the reference to the Spanish economy as 'it', and by referring to the complex collage of human behaviour as markets who manifest characteristics that can only apply to independent phenomena, such as forgetfulness and concentration. This first assumption represents an initial stage of reification and demonstrates an 'apprehension of human phenomena as if they were things'.[11]

Secondly, a further reification of economic phenomena from the human world can be seen by the assumption that these 'things' (i.e. the markets and the Spanish economy) have characteristics (i.e. forgetfulness, concentration, the capacity to be 'overwhelmed', the need to be shored up, and the state of 'growth') that are generally reserved for living phenomena. This creates an impression of economic phenomena as living organisms with a wide array of human characteristics, such as the capacity for independent agency and states of consciousness.

Consider the following example taken from an article on the American stock market:

> In February pay rolls expanded by over 200,000 for the third successive month. Retail sales rose at their fastest pace in five months.

The notions of pay roll expanding and retail sales rising at their fastest pace lend the phenomena under consideration a materiality, as they create a spatial impression.

Describing economic phenomena as having the same capacities and characteristics as material objects (being able to expand and move at a fast pace) reinforces the notion that the 'economy' is a thing with its own semi-corporal 'ontological status independent of human activity and signification.'[12]

The following example is taken from an article on the Greek economy:

> The collective sigh of relief that rippled through international markets following the latest election in Greece was almost audible.

In this instance 'international markets' are capable of producing an 'almost audible' 'sigh of relief'. I realise of course that the characteristics that these examples attribute to economic phenomena are metaphorical, and that upon reading the above quotation no one would actually imagine a physical thing called 'the international markets' sighing with relief. However, given the extremely abstract and contestable nature of economic phenomena, and the general lack of public knowledge about the economy, describing such phenomena as having autonomous human characteristics does lead to a certain iterative metaphorical conception of them.

The following quote from the magazine neatly illustrates the manner in which much of media discourse nurtures a conception of the economy as a natural phenomenon that abides by its own rules:

> The economy depends about as much on economists as the weather does on weather forecasters.

Drawing an analogy between the economy and the weather is pertinent as it implicitly suggests that the economy is so alienated from human control and activity that it is something we must react to, in the same way that we react to the weather.

If we think about the marketing pressure to either shock or excite people into purchasing future products, it becomes easy to put the vision of the economy outlined above into context. The visceral and exciting physicality derived from imagining the economy in this fashion allows one to write about it as an object of great autonomous power. The mantra of fear and greed that underlies much of the discourse manifests through the representation of the economy as a powerful creature which we must react to (e.g. – a Bull or a Bear). Fear and greed, rather than being the central emotions that propel and define the economy in a self-fulfilling or performative fashion, instead become reactions to it, to 'the economy', as a natural autonomous entity.

By continuously depicting one phenomenon in the lexicon of another (our economy/an autonomous natural creature), the discursive referents of that phenomenon become saturated with different meanings and shared reference points.[13] The categories of the economy and nature become mixed with the constant metaphorical depiction of the economy as a natural entity, further distancing it from political or human control and pushing it into the realm of autonomous agency.

This vision of the economy suits the exclusive community who produce it. By presenting the economy as a beast that can't be tamed, there is an implication that the economy is a natural phenomenon arising of its own accord. It is not something that is determined or controlled by political or human actions, but by a natural hierarchy. This masks the very man-made laws and institutions that do in fact structure and determine how our economy works, as well as who benefits from it and who doesn't.

Furthermore, depicting the economy as a natural entity plays into the trope of the free market being an expression of human nature. For advocates of the free market, the natural driving force behind our economy is our desire to look out for number one: 'It is not from the benevolence of the butcher, the brewer, or the baker that we expect our dinner, but from their regard to their own interest'.[14] So runs the most used quotation in economic theory, used to justify a market system that harnesses our natural tendency to put ourselves first. From this perspective, government intervention not only messes with the ability to make profits, it is also against our nature, and ultimately the nature of the economy.

The economy as an investment opportunity

Reifying the economy as an autonomous natural entity helps those writing about it present it as an investment opportunity, as it aids the idea that you can learn about this 'beast' and work out what it might do next. This is important, as the central purpose of the discourse in *Money Matters* is that it is a product, and as a product its value stems from its capacity to tell investors what they should or should not do with their money. This is true not just for the one magazine I visited but for the vast majority of economic coverage in the media.

Money Matters advertised itself as offering the 'very best market analysis and financial insights from the sharpest financial minds in Britain' and as 'Invaluable reading for anyone with a retirement lump sum to invest'. One impact this has had on the discourse was demonstrated earlier in the chapter, in the discussion of the need for the discourse to be opinionated, as evidenced in the lengthy quote from the co-founder, who explained that the magazine only became successful once it started adopting firm positions rather than acting as a digest. In the discourse generated by this stance, events in all their local complexities do not need detailed analysis; instead, the world is imagined in terms of its implications for the balance-sheets of investors.

Kantola's work on *The Financial Times*'s coverage of elections shows the political implications this generalising discourse has. Her extensive analysis demonstrates that in the pages of the *Financial Times*, liberal free-market economic reform is presented as inevitable and placed above democratic principles. She states that:

> As this unifying and deterritorialized language is losing its links with everyday reality and local circumstances, it is used primarily for governing spaces with a globalized imaginary of productivism, which belittles the local polities and democracies as nuisances for the inevitable advance of the global economy.[15]

Kantola's work shows that local contexts are ignored within a vision that prioritises the interests of an investing class. In this vision, people's everyday economic lives disappear from view as they are subsumed by a discourse that focuses on productivity and profits. It is worth quoting the seminal work of linguists Lackoff and Johnson on metaphor at length here, as they sum up the point far better than I can:

> When we accept the LABOUR AS A RESOURCE metaphor and assume that the cost of resources defined in this way should be kept down, then cheap labour becomes a good thing, on a par with cheap oil. The exploitation of human beings through this metaphor is most obvious in countries that boast of 'a virtually inexhaustible supply of cheap labour' – a neutral sounding economic statement that hides the reality of human degradation ... The blind acceptance of the metaphor can hide degrading realities.[16]

Mythologising the economy as an investment opportunity or simply as a place to make money leads to headlines like:

> 'How to escape the most hated tax in Britain' – your comprehensive, easy-to-follow, step-by-step guide containing everything you need to know to protect up to £2 million of your money from inheritance tax.

The complexities of inheritance, its role in maintaining and increasing structural inequality, the local meanings given to it in specific contexts and the manner in which taxing it supports social institutions – is washed away by this depiction, as it is seen simply as something to avoid.

There are ideological implications behind imagining the economy as an investment opportunity, as it focuses in on one aspect and brackets out other realties. As such, like the notion of the economy as an autonomous beast, mythologising the economy as an investment opportunity pushes the economic discourse in the media away from the reality of most people and towards an exclusive community – i.e. those with enough money to invest.

Mythologising the economy as both an investment opportunity and as an autonomous natural entity aids the overarching myth of the economy as a pot of money. Firstly, as discussed in chapter 3, on economic myth in the political sphere, reifying the economy as an autonomous entity facilitates the idea that it is something we must respond to – something that controls us, rather than something we control, something like the existential restraint of a household budget, or a pot of money.

Secondly, the notion of the economy as an investment opportunity generates a vison of it as pot of money, with market logic directing how it is distributed through investment. This vision brackets out any consideration of the structural powers that determine where money comes from and how it is allocated. Instead, it helps facilitate the idea outlined in chapter 2 on the financial sphere – that finance's role is to distribute the pot in the most efficient manner possible, and, as argued in that chapter, this feeds into the notion that the economy consists of a finite amount of money, which needs, one way or another, to be allocated.

If the media is the main source of economic information that people engage with, and the crucial bridge between elites and the broader public, then it's possible to see why there is such a disconnect when it comes to the economy. On the one hand, you have a select wealthy few who engage with a media discourse that is tailored for them, and prioritises investment advice and a vision of the economy that serves that community. Much airtime and many words are devoted to this group, and the journalists serving it have no incentive to follow the democratic ideals outlined at the start of the chapter: keeping a check on elites, informing the public, and acting as a mode of communication between elites and the public.

On the other hand, you have the vast majority of people, who are excluded from this discourse and are ill equipped to deal with the scant level of economic coverage that comes their way. Journalists working on stories for the broader public face the difficult task of trying to tell the story they are covering in the most engaging fashion, while also trying to educate an audience who have very little prior understanding of the economy. All the while they are struggling under the difficult business context outlined at the start of the chapter, which leaves them less time for each story and pushes them towards a sensationalism that is ill fitting for serious coverage.

On top of this, like the civil servants in chapter 3, journalists work in strictly hierarchal institutions and are under pressure to present a vision of the world that pleases their proprietors, who have an interest in maintaining the status quo and are often deeply connected to the financial world. This, combined with the need to appeal to an audience of investors, leads to a vision of the economy emanating from the financial press that parrots the myth already present in financial institutions they are reporting on or to.

At the heart of this myth is the idea of the economy as an autonomous natural entity whose movements experts can predict. And it is from selling their expert knowledge of this beast that the financial media, as well as much of the financial world, makes its money. However, even if we subscribe to the notion of the economy as this wild beast, there are some questions to be raised over the ability of these experts in the media and in the City of London to predict how it moves.

Take, for instance, the rise in passive funds discussed in chapter 2. These funds simply track the market index; they rely on no expert information or specialist knowledge, but just passively follow the market. If we compare the success of these funds with those run by the experts who pour over the evidence and tell you what the yield on Danish sovereign debt is going to be, or on whether or not you should buy gold, it's possible to see that, since 2007, these passive funds have been four times more profitable than those run by the specialists.[17] Indeed, a report from 2020 found that 90% of actively managed funds had failed to beat the market over the previous 15 years.[18]

What this shows is that these experts, who actively seek to manage money by using their specialist knowledge, do not even come close to breaking even with what would happen if they just spread their money out across the market. They are on average 90% worse. If these expert fund managers can't get it right, what hope does a financial journalist, or indeed, the retail punter they are trying to advise, have? The words of the one of the *Money Matters* senior editors becomes salient in light of this statistic– 'an ounce of passion is worth a ton of fact'.

Ultimately, economic discourse in the media is caught up in the system it is supposed to pass comment on. It is part of the same industry that profits on claims to knowledge about the economy, regardless of the basis of those claims. These claims, and the language they are made in, keep the world of finance spinning, and help proliferate the dangerous myth about our economy that I have outlined in the pages above.

5

Demythologising the economy: not a pot of money

Due to pure good luck, I found myself, in my late twenties, to be the owner of a flat in London. It was an unusually decorated large mezzanine studio, in a relatively deprived area. During that time (2013–2017), I worked in a pub, as a football coach, and occasionally as an associate lecturer, while trying to complete my PhD. I owned that flat for four years. It was a nice flat, except for the quasi-criminal freeholder, who made a number of thinly veiled threats against my personhood.

I was earning around £12,000 a year from the part-time work, along with occasionally renting the flat out through Airbnb, and my partner was supporting me by paying some rent. However, the flat increased in value by around £120,000 over those four years. £40,000 a year!

During that period the average wage in the UK was around £28,000. There is a serious problem with an economic system that pays the owner of a property to sit around in his pants (not what I was doing all the time) – considerably more than what most people get for devoting 42 hours a week / most of their waking life, to a job.

This problem is deeply connected to the pot of money myth as it concerns the question of how money is created and allocated.

Money for nothing

A recent poll of 100 MPs demonstrated that 71% wrongly believed that: 'Only the government – via the Bank of England or Royal Mint – has the authority to create money, including coins, notes and the electronic money in your bank account'.[1] However, in fact less than 3% of money in the UK has been created by the government.[2]

Figure 3 illustrates the exponential growth in money created by privately owned banks (M4) from the 1960s onwards and compares it to the base money (money created by the government):

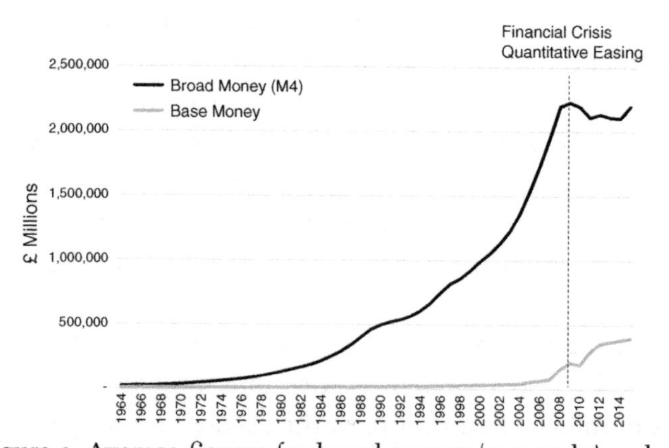

Figure 3 Average figures for broad money (quarterly) and base money (monthly), 1964–2014
Source: based on data from the Federal Reserve, Bank of St Louis, https://fred.stlouisfed.org/tags/series?t=monetary+aggregates%3Bunited+kingdom (accessed 31 March 2021).

Money supply: base money and broad money (M4)

As Figure 3 shows, the money in our society is created mainly by private organisations. The result of this is that private organisations with the capacity to create money determine how wealth is allocated across society. There is strong evidence to indicate that when allocating money these institutions favour investments that are non-productive, and invest in existing assets that do not add to GDP.[3] The recent unprecedented inflation in the housing market and the astronomical growth of trading on the foreign exchange market and in fixed assets and securities amongst banks are testament to this. To reiterate this point, it is worth remembering that only around 3% of the money loaned out by the banking system in the UK is lent to firms engaged in the production of goods or services (i.e. to industries that employ people).[4]

Figure 4 (overleaf) indicates the discrepancy between GDP and money supply following financial deregulation in the mid-1980s. This has two important implications regarding the vision of the economy as a 'pot of money' or household budget. First, the efficient market hypothesis is a myth because the financial sector and the financial markets do not allocate capital to the places that need it and will use it productively – which is key to their self-professed reason for existence.[5] Second, the 'common-sense' notion that underpins the justification for austerity (and was prevalent on the estate), that the government operates under the same laws that would apply to a household budget, needs to be seriously

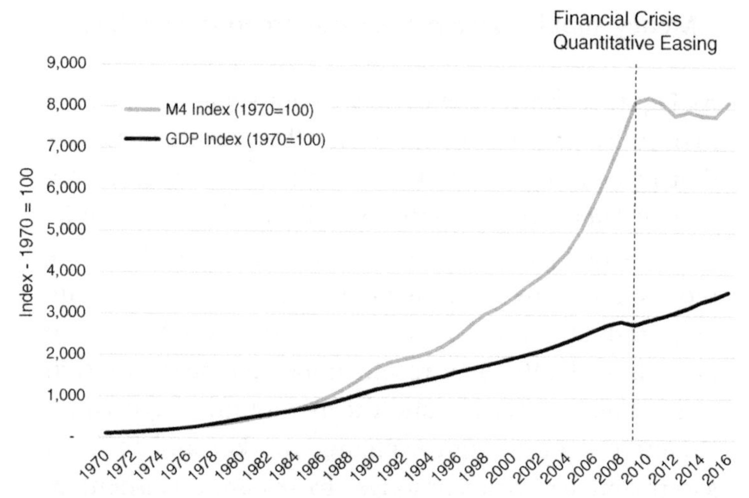

Figure 4 Broad money (M4) and nominal GDP indexed from 1970
Source: based on data from: Office for National Statistics, *Gross Domestic Product at Market Prices: Current Prices: Seasonally Adjusted* (2021), www.ons.gov.uk/economy/grossdomesticproductgdp/timeseries/ybha/pn2; The Bank of England Interactive database, M4 (Code LPQAUYN) (accessed 29 March 2021).

questioned. It clearly needs to take into account how money is created.

Readers who are new to the notion of credit creation may find it strange that private firms can create money from nowhere. Yet the process is accepted by mainstream economists and respected commentators like *The Financial Times*'s Martin Wolf, who writes: 'The essence of the contemporary monetary system is the creation of money, out of nothing, by private banks' often foolish lending'.[6] In order to get to the bottom of how this works, and to illustrate why the economy is not a 'pot of money', it is worth taking some time here to explore a more or less standard account of the money creation process.

A brief history of money

Different forms of private money creation have existed for millennia,[7] but the version that characterises the contemporary scene in the UK is best understood by going back to the goldsmiths of the seventeenth century. The second half of the seventeenth century was a time of war and insecurity, so people wanted safe houses to store their precious metals (usually gold). Goldsmiths, who had secure spaces to store such valuables, began to earn money by acting as safety deposit holders.[8] They had secure safes that were trusted storage spaces and charged people a small price for keeping their valuables in them.

When a customer deposited something in a goldsmith's safe, the goldsmith would issue them with a receipt, which could be used to withdraw the deposit in the future. As this practice became widespread, depositors started to pay for things with deposit receipts, thus transferring ownership of the deposit to the seller. To facilitate this payment system, more and more unnamed deposit receipts were issued by goldsmiths, until eventually they became a generally accepted means of payment: paper money.

For goldsmiths, this presented a further business opportunity. They were amassing larger and larger quantities of gold, which were lying dormant in their safes, and they realised that they could lend out some of the gold and charge interest on it. The interest would be pure profit for the goldsmiths at almost no cost. To counter the risk of loaning out the gold, they had to ensure that they lent against collateral which they would be able to collect if the loan wasn't repaid. So, they started to loan out gold at small rates of interest against collateral.

Then another development occurred. Given that the receipts were an accepted means of payment, they realised that they could give borrowers deposit receipts instead of gold. They could print deposit receipts (even if they did not relate to any deposited gold) and loan them out, charging interest.

If all went well, the goldsmiths would collect their interest and be repaid in full, but if the debtor failed to pay, the goldsmiths could foreclose and collect the collateral. It was fraud (as there was often no gold backing up the receipts), but also a win-win situation for the goldsmiths. The economist Richard Werner (quoting his colleague Withers) writes of this process: 'Banking was born: the same process describes the activity of present-day commercial banks: "some ingenious goldsmith conceived the epoch-making notion of giving notes not only to those who had deposited metal, but also to those who came to borrow it, and so founded modern banking"'.[9]

The story doesn't quite end there. In time, central banks were established, and the issuance of paper money (i.e. banknotes or deposit receipts) by private firms was outlawed. Only central banks (which were often connected to governments) were allowed to print paper money or mint coins, as policy makers sought to control the supply and allocation of money. However, while it remains the case that commercial banks cannot issue physical banknotes or coins, there is nothing to stop them typing numbers on computer screens and creating digital money. As such, digitisation, combined with deregulation in the mid- and latter part of the twentieth century, and the move away from the gold standard (Bretton woods) has led to an enormous resurgence in private bank money over the past five decades (see Figure 4). To reiterate, currently about 97% of the UK's money supply is created by private banks.

The fact that private organisations can (and do) control the supply of money would seem intuitively wrong to many people – and perhaps for good reason, as private banks don't just create almost all of the money in our society, they also, through their lending and other decisions, determine how it is allocated. You don't need a Nobel Prize in economics, or even an economics degree, to recognise that the institutions that create and allocate the vast majority of money in a society (like the kings and queens of old), will have significant power over the shape of that society.[10]

Private credit creation means that private institutions are able to determine which sectors of society receive money and which don't – or 'who gets what and what goes were'. It will not have escaped the reader's attention that over the past 40 years or so some things have become far more profitable than others. Working, for instance, has not been particularly profitable, whilst owning a property has been extremely profitable (especially for those, like myself, in London and the South East where property prices have risen fastest). This is the difference between what economists call income (the money you are paid for doing your job) and wealth (the value of the assets you own). Consider that in 1980 the average wage in the UK was £4,542,[11] with the average house price at £19,273,[12] while in 2021 the average wage is £31,461[13] and the average house price is £231,855.[14] This shows that house prices have grown at almost twice the rate of wages: see the crazy disparity between wages and house prices in Figure 5.

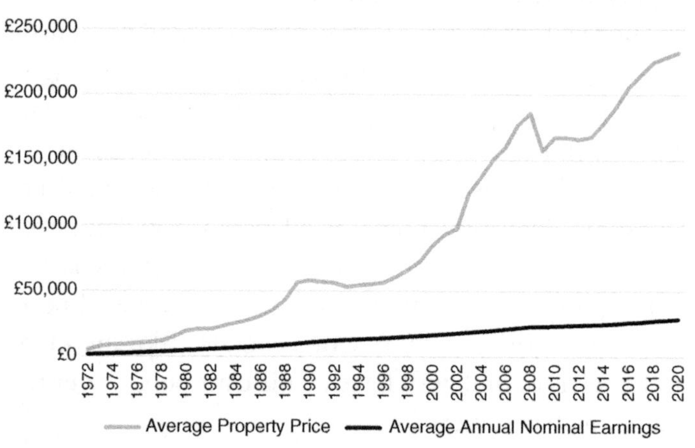

Figure 5 Salaries versus house prices, 1972–2020
Source: based on data from: gov.uk, 'UK House Price Index' (14 August 2019), www.gov.uk/government/statistical-data-sets/uk-house-price-index-data-downloads-june-2019; G. Clark, 'What Were the British Earnings and Prices Then?' (2021), www.measuringworth.com/ukearncpi/ (accessed 31 March 2021).

The implications are that the people who own houses, like those who own other assets,[15] have become richer as the value of their assets has increased substantially, while those who don't and have to work for a living get left behind.

Now consider that of all of the money created by the British banking system, only around 3% goes as loans to firms or individuals engaged in the production of goods or services[16] (firms that pay wages). The rest of it goes towards non-productive assets like different forms of property or paper coupons like shares or bonds that are often used for speculation.[17] This begs the question: why would private credit creators put money into static non-productive assets, rather than into firms and businesses that employ people to make or do things? Because, like the goldsmiths in the seventeenth century, credit creators want to lend against collateral: if you lend to a business that makes things or carries out services, then you are counting on repayment from a future income stream produced by product sales; but if it all goes wrong and they can't repay, there won't be much collateral for you to collect. However, if you lend on property (residential or commercial) or various kinds of bonds and the borrower can't repay, you can take ownership of their property.

So, in a system in which private institutions driven by the profit motive create and allocate money as they see fit, there is a clear incentive to pump money into fixed assets that can be taken as collateral. If these assets are owned by an already wealthy minority, then the effect is to make them even richer, and to drive inequality by attracting investment away from the 'real' productive economy of goods and services, from which the majority of the population draws income and relies on to survive. The asset distribution in our society means that at present, wealth inequality is about twice as great as income inequality on some measures,[18] with around 10% of the population owning 50% of the wealth, and the average net wealth for the lowest 40% being 0.[19]

This system is behind what Bret Christopher calls 'rentier capitalism',[20] as it propels a situation in which the ownership of assets, rather than the creation of goods and services becomes the central determinant in the allocation of wealth and power across society.[21] By driving up asset prices, it allows those who own them to capitalise on their increased worth, and to profit on the use of these assets by those who cannot afford to own them.[22] As such, it is a key factor in the rising levels of inequality we have seen for the past 40 years or so.[23]

Furthermore, as the scenario with the goldsmiths outlined above indicates, when bankers create money by lending they also create debt, as borrowers are expected to pay that money back. A system that depends on debt is one that is likely to be prone to boom-bust cycles (as there will be greedy periods of reckless lending and then fearful periods of paying some of that lending back). The most recent example was the crisis of 2008, when huge quantities of money that had been issued by banks created a global financial system that was entirely dependent on debt. When it became evident that some of that debt wasn't going to be paid back and some of the assets used as collateral weren't sufficient, trust was lost, the flows of credit and lending stopped and the system seized up. Money that had been flooding into institutions, industries and whole countries was suddenly withdrawn, creating social, political and economic chaos.[24]

Linked to the boom-bust cycles intrinsic to an economy dependent on private debt, and the surge in investment in fixed assets, is a tendency towards speculation. As a result of the incentive to invest in static assets, the value of those assets increases, making them even more appealing. Profit-seeking credit creators then pump more money into these assets, thinking they will be able to sell them at a later date for a higher price. Hence stock market bubbles, like the current one which is leading to the boom in what are called SPACs (special purpose acquisition companies). These are firms without operating activities that use pooled investor funds to buy a firm whose activity is not known to the promoters and certainly not disclosed to initial investors.[25] Although investors do not know what they will invest in (the SPAC promoters will decide that at a later date), they invest regardless in the hope of profit. Speculation like this, along with the debt financing described above, leads to instability, as when something else comes along and money is moved from one asset to another, the value of the initial asset begins to fall. There is then a rush to get money out of one area and into another, which provokes a harmful instability.

Finally, there is no incentive for private firms to invest in social goods, like education, healthcare or green infrastructure. Investment in these areas often does not produce an income stream in return, so there is no reason a private firm, driven by the profit motive, would seek to invest in them. As such, an economy dominated by private credit creation underfunds these areas of social overhead expenditure, making healthcare and education more expensive for the average citizen. At the same time, fund investors and major corporates pump money into fossil fuel, high carbon industries, aggravating the climate emergency.

I have sketched, in the broadest of terms, some of the problems that arise in a system that is dependent on the creation of private money: it is a system that breeds inequality as it generates private affluence and public squalor while aggravating environmental crisis. These problems are structural and institutional; they have nothing to do with issuing a finite pot of money, but stem from who has the power to create and distribute money.

Controlling the money supply

There is some recognition of these problems among policy makers, and, as such, the state does attempt to exert some control over the money-creation process. However, the three policies they traditionally use are ineffective at controlling private credit creation and allocation in any meaningful way. I will outline the issues here. Those who want a more detailed account should refer to the more scholarly and expert work of system critics like Pettifor, Ryan-Collins et al. and Werner:[26]

1. *The formal regulatory tool (e.g. the ability to set reserve requirement).* Rather than gold, cash and central bank reserves, which are created by the central bank and issued to private banks, are now used as the reserve behind the private credit that banks create. The reserve requirement is the amount of reserves a bank needs in relation to the deposit accounts it has created for its customers. When customers physically take out cash from a commercial bank they take out notes that the bank has received from the central bank. In principle, a central bank (or government) can introduce a regulation that means that commercial banks must have a ratio of reserves in relation to the money they create in deposit accounts. In this way the central bank could control how much money is created by commercial banks, as the central bank is the only place reserves can be created. In reality, following deregulation in the early 1970s the Bank of England abolished the need for commercial banks to have a minimum level of reserves in relation to their total deposits. There have been some attempts to reintroduce it following the 2008 crisis, but there is a fear that if ratio levels are increased there will be a liquidity crisis (i.e. the banks will not be able to provide customers with their deposits). Instead, the policy

has been to create more reserves to match the already inflated credit.[27]

2. *The quantity tool (ability to manipulate the amount of reserves).* Rather than setting reserve ratios for each bank, central banks can simply increase or decrease the amount of reserves in the system. In principle, this will have the knock-on effect of increasing or decreasing the amount of money commercial banks are willing to deposit in customers' accounts. However, there are a number of reasons as to why this is ineffective. Firstly, issuance of reserves tends to follow rather than lead commercial bank created money. This is because if the central bank does not issue reserves when a commercial bank needs them to, the entire payment system may collapse, which would have detrimental effects on society at large. So, ultimately, the central bank will provide reserves if the commercial banking sector needs them to. As Ryan-Collins et al. state: 'When a commercial bank requests additional central bank reserves or cash, the Bank of England is not in a position to refuse'.[28] So, the 'quantity tool' is ineffective in regards to its ability to restrict credit creation. Furthermore, if the central bank wishes to issue more reserves to increase bank credit creation and stimulate economic activity (as it may wish to do in times of recession), the result may well prove to be ineffective, as there is no guarantee that banks will spend their excess

capacity if they do not trust the market. They might just sit on those new reserves or, as is happening with QE, they may elect to use their extra spending power to allocate money to non-productive assets, which do not contribute to the betterment of society but only push asset prices up. Thirdly, and the final major reason reserve ratios are ineffective in the current scenario, is rather than having to always settle up with each other in central bank reserves, commercial banks can net out with each other in the money they create. What this means is that if bank A creates £100 and gives it to bank B, and then bank B creates £100 and gives it to bank A, both banks will be even and there will be no need to transfer central bank reserves. Money will have been created irrespective of central bank reserves, so if all the banks create money at the same time, total money will increase regardless of what the central bank does.[29]

3. *Interest rates.* In the UK and across other industrialised nations, starting in the early 1970s, there was a move away from trying to directly control the quantity of credit created by commercial banks and towards controlling the price of credit – i.e. towards controlling interest rates. Central banks thought that by controlling the price banks could borrow reserves at, they would be able to control the price at which banks lend to each other and to their customers, and thus have some control over the amount of money in the economy. Higher

interest rates would mean less people would want to borrow money and less money would be created; lower interest rates would mean that more people would want to borrow and more money would be created. However, Lee and Werner[30] draw on empirical evidence from the US, the UK, Germany and Japan to show that rather than determining or controlling credit, interest rates follow credit growth or depletion. So again, the tail seems to be wagging the dog. Further to this, as Pettifor[31] has shown, the interest rate set by the Bank of England has very little effect on the interest rates set in the 'real' economy because the Bank's rate has been lowering over time while the real interest rate (the rates at which businesses and individuals borrow) has been rising over time. Furthermore, as is evidenced by the experience in the UK and in Japan over the past few decades, low interest rates do not mean that banks will lend (create) more money. As Werner[32] has argued, banks lend (create), depending on whether or not they think they will be paid back or on the collateral behind the loan, rather than on the interest they hope to receive. As a central bank tool for controlling bank credit creation, setting the interest rate at which banks can borrow reserves has little effect. Finally, even if central banks were successful in their attempt to control the supply of money through interest rates, they would still be unable to control how the money was allocated, and therefore would be unable to stem the allocation of money towards unproductive, speculative or environmentally damaging means and direct it towards productive purposes that benefit society.

Taking back control

So, private firms have a relatively free hand in creating our societies' money and deciding where it goes. This is problematic, as the arguments above have demonstrated. However, reform is possible and there are things that can be done to change the situation. If we recognise this and start to do some of these things, whole new futures become visible.

For instance, one shock treatment method for regaining control over the money creation process would be to ban private credit creation altogether. Banks would therefore only be able to lend out the money their customers have deposited with them, which is how most people think banks work anyway. This would massively rein in their ability to pump money into unproductive assets.

However, placing a ban on credit creation in the institutions that create 97% of our money is a draconian policy, and the effective withdrawal of established credit lines would have a huge immediate shock effect on all kinds of economic activity, which would dwarf any previous banking crisis. One different option, among others less radical,[33] would be to increase the percentage of central bank reserves commercial banks are required to have in relation to the loans and deposits they make. Indeed, up until the late 1960s, UK banks had to hold 8% of their assets in the form of cash and had to have a liquidity/reserve ratio of 28–32%.[34] This restrains credit creation as reserves can only be created by the central bank, thus allowing the policy makers a degree of control over the amount of money created. Some advocates of this approach think that banks should ultimately have 100% reserves for all the money they lend out or deposit; this would give the central bank total control over how much money is in the system and effectively be a ban on private credit creation.[35]

Increasing the reserve ratio or banning credit creation altogether would rein in the ability of private organisations to create money and add some stability to our economic system. But these solutions don't deal with inequality or the climate crisis, as they don't deal with the allocation of money – with the issue of 'what goes where and who gets what'.

Yet there are many practical and historical examples of money being created and directed towards more productive and socially beneficial ends. For instance, in Germany regional saving banks known as Sparkassen have a mandate for public service and local development. As such, they are responsible to their local municipalities, and prioritise lending that benefits society. A large part of this is a focus on productive lending and they provide the finance for 70% of Germany's much envied SME (small to median enterprise) sector.[36] Furthermore, because of their social mandate, which is decreed in Germany's constitution, they are 'significant contributors' to the movement towards a green transition.[37]

The same sort of system could easily be applied in the UK. Think of the benefits that would have occurred if the £500 billion the state created as part of its QE programme after the 2008 financial crisis had been allocated towards green and other socially beneficial projects rather than handed over to the financial sector and then pumped into static assets. Furthermore, as we have witnessed throughout the COVID-19 pandemic, it is relatively straightforward for the state to create money and direct it to the places that need it.

Other high-profile examples of policy makers influencing the creation and allocation of money include: the UK up until the late 1960s, as banks were given ceilings on how much they could lend and also told where they should lend to;[38] the Fed in the 1920s; the Japanese, Korean and Taiwanese systems from the 1940s onwards, and present-day China. Richard Werner's highly regarded book on Japan[39] shows how the Japanese post-war 'miracle' growth was achieved through policy makers controlling and directing bank credit creation. As he puts it in a later work: 'Essentially, the central bank told the private banks on a quarterly basis by how much they would increase their lending' and adds that the central bank also told the private banks which sectors of the economy to lend to.[40]

Again, I am writing as an outsider and drawing on the work of established economists and system critics like Werner. But, as the last few paragraphs show, there are historical examples and strong precedents which demonstrate practical ways in which we could shift the control of the production and allocation of credit away from private organisations and towards a more productive, socially constructive, greener and fairer way of doing things. These ideas are gaining traction in the world of economic theory, but have little chance of making it into the mainstream if the institutions I visited – institutions that should be educating and informing the public about the economy – continue to perpetuate myth.

Modern monetary theory

Moving credit creation away from private firms means moving it towards the control of our democratically elected government, which raises further points of discussion.

Firstly, there is a widespread view that the state can't just create money out of nowhere, as it is limited in how much it can spend by how much tax it collects and how much money it borrows. Secondly, there is a fear that if the state could just turn on the printing press, there would be rampant inflation, as they would succumb to the political pressure to create more and more money.

However, an increasingly influential branch of economics known as modern monetary theory (MMT) argues that states who are in control of their own currency can create as much money as they want, and can do so without causing inflation as long as there is unused economic capacity and some unemployment of labour. This is because central banks or treasuries can always type more zeros onto their computer screens and then send those zeros to somewhere in the economy. MMT argues that this works because governments are currency issuers rather than currency users,[41] and as long as the currency they issue has value in their society (which it is likely to as it is the currency that they collect tax in) they can determine the money supply and issue as much or little as they want. As such, according to MMT, once the important caveats about available resources have been established,[42] there is no budget constraint: governments who are in control of their own currency do not have to only spend what they tax or borrow, they can, and do (QE), create money out of nowhere.

So, if this is true, and governments can create money out of nowhere, why don't they create more of it to do things like buy medical equipment for our hospitals, build houses and pay nurses or teachers more? Inflation. More money being pumped into a system in which there is already full employment of resources, and therefore a limited quantity of goods and services, just produces general inflation and widespread higher prices: people will be paid more, but things will cost more, and nothing much will have changed.

However, as things stand, private banks create and allocate almost all our money and this has led to inflation of some prices but not of others. As explained above, we have seen inflation in housing and other fixed assets, but little change in the wages people get paid or in the everyday things they spend their money on. This type of inflation, driven by private credit creators, clearly benefits wealthy asset holders at the cost of the rest of society.

Yet the pandemic provides a good example of why government spending, as opposed to private credit creation, doesn't need to be inflationary, and can be socially beneficial. Consider that, since the beginning of the pandemic, the government has poured £450 billion into the economy, but we have seen no real inflation. This is because the money the government spent was targeted towards picking up the slack from private sector closure (i.e. providing income for workers and firms who were idle) in an economy which had masses of unused resources. As such, it shows that putting money into unused resources does not create inflation. And this implies that running the economy at less than full capacity (e.g. full employment) creates room for government spending that won't be inflationary. A key aspect of this from an MMT perspective is that the government wouldn't need to pay back any of the money because they didn't borrow it from anywhere, but simply printed it from scratch.[43]

MMT's arguments do not only insist that the state can step in and spend money in areas where there are unused resources, they also highlight that through regaining control of the money supply the state gains the opportunity to move resources from one sector of the economy to another, as through tax and spending the government can move money around different sectors of the economy without causing inflation. For example, the state could engineer higher pay for care workers, teachers or nurses by creating money and directing it towards those sectors, and developing legislation that meant that it translated into higher wages. While at the same time, if they were worried about the inflationary impact such a policy would have, they could raise taxes on the incomes of those who work in less socially beneficial jobs, such as wholesale finance. This would result in a shift of resources, from those working in finance to those working in socially beneficial sectors. It would not lead to inflation or deflation as it would be a case of taking money away from one area and adding it to another. What MMT argues is that the government is much freer in its capacity to move money around the system like this than many people believe, as its spending will not be dependent upon how much it taxes or borrows. As such, it could both pay care workers more and invest in green infrastructure without raising taxes anywhere else, if it felt there was space in the economy to do so without causing undue inflation.[44]

I have only sketched some of the MMT positions because they represent the 'pot of money' myth turned upside down by economically literate radicals within the profession. I would encourage the reader to look up more serious accounts, like Fullbrook and Morgan, Kelton or Ryan-Collins et al.[45] And note that the pandemic has so far lent credibility to the MMT approach.

In total, the pandemic has seen the Bank of England (a publicly owned body) create and then pump £450 billion into our economy;[46] the Fed have spent close to $6 trillion.[47] If the economy was a pot of money, the huge deficit spending and the enforced closure of large sections of the private sector would have emptied it and led to utter havoc – empty shelves, rationing, mass unemployment, pitchforks at the door. But the economy isn't a pot of money: at the time of writing, the unemployment rate is no worse than it was at the start of 2016, and the stock market has had a bumper year.

The reason we are still standing is that the government have covered the tab. In creating more money, the state did what it always has had the capacity to do – it took over from a failing private sector. This included paying the wages of close to 10 million furloughed workers.[48]

So, there is a strong argument for querying the restraint that comes with the idea that the state can only spend what it taxes and borrows (the political version of the pot of money myth). Then, it becomes possible to see how, through re-gaining control of the money supply, the state could build a much fairer and greener economy.

Indeed, it could be argued that central banks have already been practising a version of MMT for a number of years. The QE programme that was set up after the 2008 crisis involves the central bank creating money and then buying government bonds from private financial firms.[49] The effect is to place the newly created money (£895 billion to date),[50] into the hands of the private financial firms, who are then free to spend it how they wish. This was necessary after the 2008 financial crisis, as the financial system was on the verge of collapse and needed the prop of state-created money. So, the central bank is already creating money and directing it towards a certain area of our economy (finance). QE and the pandemic give the lie to the 'pot of money' myth; they show to anyone who takes the time to look into them that established Western democracies who are in control of their own currencies can, when they feel it necessary, create vast sums of money out of thin air and allocate that money wherever they choose.

Yet, despite this firepower to create money out of nothing at the state's disposal, we are already beginning to hear the murmurings of austerity: that we will need to pay it all back in the post-pandemic world; that there is no magic money tree and we will need to suffer, to tighten our belts. Recognising that the economy is not a 'pot of money' allows us to see through this dangerous myth, and opens up the possibility of thinking about a different future.

The three elite spaces I have looked at (finance, government, media) endorse and project a vison of the economy as a detached, depersonalised and autonomous entity, and this facilitates the myth of the economy as something akin to a pot of money. But, as argued above, the financial sector creates and distributes money and credit under laws and regulations which are not part of some de-historicised 'natural' logic.[51] Under a different set of laws and regulations, the situation would be different, the sector would not have the power it has today, and the economy would not look like it does today. As such, rather than reifying the economy as an autonomous quasi-natural entity, it would be better to think of it as almost entirely dependent on laws and regulations – laws and regulations that, for the vast majority of the population, are unseen, as they are lost in the fog of myth that shrouds our economy.

While the people I spoke to on the estate did not see the economy as governed by a depersonalised autonomous logic, but as an entity the rich controlled for their own benefit, they nevertheless did reify it as something akin to a pot of money.

However, this doesn't square with the reality of credit creation outlined above. Private banks create money when they want to and the government can do the same. Think of QE: while the people in my neighbourhood were saying to me, there 'just isn't enough money in the pot to go round', the government were pumping billions of newly created money into the financial sector. The capacity was there, as it always is, for the state to create more money. As shown by the reaction to the COVID-19 crisis, if we need it, the money is there. Therefore, it's inaccurate to view the economy as something that is built up by people paying their taxes and then emptied out by immigrants, refugees and lazy youths. Instead, we need a vision that can incorporate the fact of credit creation.

The pot of money myth in the financial sector took the form of the pot as something that the sector, following market logic, was best placed to allocate, along with the idea that the sector filled the pot up through paying / allocating tax for the rest of society to empty/spend. Yet, the fact that the sector creates money rather than allocates it, undermines this myth, as there is something very different about allocating money from a pre-determined amount (like a household budget) compared with allocating money that you have created. Furthermore, the fact that just 3% of the money the sector allocates/creates goes to firms that produce goods and services makes a mockery of the myth that it provides a service to society by efficiently distributing capital.

In the political sphere, the pot of money myth underpins the austerity narrative but does not concur with the arguments and evidence outlined above. The idea that the government can only spend what it taxes and borrows doesn't make sense when seen in the light of credit creation. QE is a textbook example of how the British state can create money whenever it likes, and just as it can create money, it can also decide where to allocate that money. In the case of QE, it has chosen to place it in the hands of the already wealthy asset holders, while at the same time taking money out of the public services much of the population rely on to survive.

The myth of the economy as a detached technical entity that I found in the civil service also falls away when we look at the facts behind how our economy works. As stated above, it is the laws and regulations that allow the financial sector the power it has to determine 'who gets what and what goes where', not some mysterious existential force or logic. Those laws and regulations are ultimately set by the government, as such reifying of the economy as a technical detached entity masks the fact that it is human and political logic that determine what it is and how it works.

As argued above, the impact on our communities of not recognising and addressing the money-creation problem is significant. In the UK the percentage of the nation's wealth controlled by the bottom 90% of the population had been steadily growing for a century up until the early 1980s, but since then it has started to decrease. Now, the richest 1% in the UK control 22% of the country's wealth.[52] In the US it's even worse. The richest 1% account for 39% of the nation's wealth.[53] At the same time, real wages haven't improved since the 1970s,[54] social services are hollowed out, public healthcare is struggling, work is precarious, and education is increasingly expensive, as our societies are becoming structured towards serving the needs of the wealthy.

That the policies which have led to this situation have been barely challenged is testament to the power of the pot of money myth. If you accept the prefabricated set of interpretations behind the myth, then there is no way to challenge the status quo; there is no way for the state to set things right because the state, like a household, is restricted by a finite budget. What has made this so outrageous over the last decade is that while this myth has been propagated, the state has been creating money and pumping it into a sector of the economy that benefits the already wealthy.

Perhaps the final word should go to David, a quantitative analysist at a hedge fund, who I spoke to over a greasy fry-up breakfast one morning on his day off. David had a PhD in physics but had left the sciences to make some money in the City. I asked him:

> Has working in the City changed the way that you think about the broader economy?

He responded:

> Oh, certainly, yes certainly. The idea of where money comes from, what is money, primarily. That's slightly disturbing to think about what's going on there ... it was quite shocking in a way to think about. Essentially, it's almost like a blueprint for exploiting people.

David, with an inquisitive and scientific mind, had seen through the myth and had been shocked by what he'd found. He'd seen how our system for creating and allocating money was a 'blueprint' for exploitation, but despite a PhD and an Oxbridge education, he had needed to see the system up close, to recognise it for what it is. Before that, he, like the rest of us, had been blinded by myth.

Just as myth behind the culture war issues gives rise to and justifies inequality based on gender, race and sexuality, economic myth gives rise to and justifies inequality and exploitation. Thankfully much energy has gone into exposing the myth behind those other types of 'cultural' inequality. In this book I have argued that the myth behind economic inequality needs to undergo the same treatment. However, for this to happen we need to have a clear-eyed, collective look at our economy. And in order for that to happen, the institutions that inform the population about the economy need to shift away from the self-serving visons I have exposed in the previous chapters, and concentrate, instead, on a new role as educators of an increasingly angry and confused public.

Notes

Introduction

1 J. F. Kennedy, *Commencement Address at Yale University* (11 June 1962).
2 I recorded conversations with 32 people working in finance.
3 I spoke with 23 civil servants in total.
4 I spoke to 32 in total.

Chapter 1 – Anger, confusion and the pot of money myth

1 OECD, 'OECD/INFE International Survey of Adult Financial Literacy Competencies' (Paris: OECD, 2016), 21, www.oecd.org/finance/OECD-INFE-International-Survey-of-Adult-Financial-Literacy-Competencies.pdf (accessed 30 March 2021).
2 A. Norrish (2017) *Exploring How People Feel About Economics – And Why We Need to Improve It*, 8, Ecnmy, www.ecnmy.org/research/report-2017/ (accessed 26 April 2021).
3 YouGov, 2015, 'YouGov/Post Crash Economics Society Survey Results', https://d25d2506sfb94s.cloudfront.net/cumulus_uploads/document/1hodojy30j/PostCrashEconomicsSocietyResults_150128_economics_W.pdf (accessed 26 April 2021).
4 D. Clarke, 'Poll Shows 85% of MPs Don't Know Where Money Comes From', Positive Money, https://positivemoney.org/2017/10/mp-poll/ (accessed 30 March 2021).

5 Further evidence of the public's 'very weak understanding' can be found in a recent report which draws on survey data and focus groups: J. Runge and N. Hudson-Sharp, *Public Understanding of Economics and Economic Statistics* (Economic Statistics Centre of Excellence, 2020), www.escoe.ac.uk/public-understanding-of-economics-and-economic-statistics/ (accessed 30 March 2021).
6 A. Killick, *Rigged: Understanding 'the Economy' in Brexit Britain* (Manchester: Manchester University Press, 2020).
7 NEON, NEF, FrameWorks Institute, PIRC, *Framing the Economy* (2017), 29, https://neweconomics.org/uploads/files/Framing-the-Economy-NEON-NEF-FrameWorks-PIRC.pdf (accessed 30 March 2021).
8 Norrish, *Exploring How People Feel About Economics.*
9 For example, G. Abbot and N. Kishtainy, *Big Ideas Simply Explained* (New York: DK Publishers, 2012); P. Krugman, *Macroeconomics* (New York: Worth Publishers, 2021); G. Mankiew, *The Principals of Economics* (New York: Harcourt, 1997).

Chapter 2 – Churches of high finance: myth in the financial sector

1 F. Norrestad, *Assets of all Financial Institutions in the United Kingdom (UK) 2002–2019* (2021) Statista, www.statista.com/statistics/421689/financial-institutions-assets-united-kingdom-uk/ (accessed 30 March 2021).
2 Bureau of Investigative Journalism, 'The Data: The Growth of City Donations to the Conservative Party' (8 February 2011), www.thebureauinvestigates.com/stories/2011-02-08/the-data-the-growth-of-city-donations-to-the-conservative-party (accessed 30 March 2021).
3 P. Geoghagan, S. Thevoz and J. Cordery, 'Revealed: The Elite Dining Club Behind 130m+ Donations to the Tories' (22 November 2019), *Open Democracy*, www.opendemocracy.net/en/dark-money-investigations/revealed-the-elite-dining-club-behind-130m-donations-to-the-tories/ (accessed 30 March 2021).
4 A. Davis, 'Whose Economy, Whose News?' in L. Basu, S. Schifferes and S. Knowles (eds) *The Media and Austerity: Comparative Perspectives* (London: Routledge, 2018).

5 M. Berry, *The Media, the Public and the Great Financial Crisis* (Basingstoke: Palgrave Macmillan, 2019).
6 See Berry, *The Media, the Public and the Great Financial Crisis*, which draws on Berry's interview material with senior economic journalists in the UK to show how advertising from the FIRE (finance, insurance and real-estate) sector, as well as the groupthink stemming from the entwinement of financial and political elites, has led to a form of media capture (242–248). For other accounts of how finance exerts influence over media coverage, see A. Davis, 'Media Effects and the Active Elite Audience: A Study of Media in Financial Markets', *European Journal of Communication* 20, no. 3 (2005): 303–326; F. Durham, 'Framing the State in Globalisation: *The Financial Times*' Coverage of the 1997 Thai Currency Crisis', *Critical Studies in Media Communication* 24, no. 1 (2007): 57–76; A. Kantola, 'On the Dark Side of Democracy: The Global Imaginary of Financial Journalism' in B. Cammaerts and N. Carpentier (eds) *Reclaiming the Media: Communication, Rights and Democratic Media Roles* (Bristol: Intellect, 2006).
7 M. Taylor, 'Financialization of Art', *Capitalism and Society* 6, no. 2 (3) (2011), https://papers.ssrn.com/sol3/papers.cfm?abstract_id=2208046 (accessed 26 April 2021).
8 Property Investor Today, 'What is the Average Cost and Size of London Homes by Borough?', www.propertyinvestortoday.co.uk/breaking-news/2019/9/what-is-the-average-cost-and-size-of-london-homes-by-borough (accessed 5 May 2021).
9 A. Tsing, *Friction: An Ethnography of Global Connection* (New Jersey: Princeton University Press, 2005).
10 D. Tuckett, *Minding the Markets: An Emotional View of Financial Instability* (London: Palgrave Macmillan, 2015).
11 J. Kay, *Other People's Money: Masters of the Universe or Servants of the People?* (London: Profile Books, 2015), 115. Kay here is echoing Keynes's (1936) famous beauty contest metaphor for equities markets. Keynes compares the markets to a beauty contest in which the judges are rewarded for selecting the most popular faces among all judges, not the one they are most attracted to. Hence, it's all about predicting who the other judges are going to vote for.
12 A. Mooney, 'Passive Funds Grow 230% to 6tn' (29 May 2016) *The Financial Times*, www.ft.com/content/2552ce62-2400-11e6-aa98-db1e01fabc0c (accessed 30 March 2021). J. Fichtner,

E. M. Heemskerk and J. Garcia-Bernardo, 'Hidden Power of the Big Three? Passive Index Funds, Re-concentration of Corporate Ownership, and New Financial Risk', *Business and Politics* 19, no. 2 (2017): 298–326.

13 J. Rosevear, 'What You Need to Know About Active vs Passive Investing' (25 March 2021) *The Motley Fool*, www.fool.com/investing/how-to-invest/active-vs-passive-investing/ (accessed 30 March 2021). J. Gittelston, 'End of an Era: Passive Equity Funds Surpass Active in Epic Shift' (11 September 2019) Bloomberg, www.bloomberg.com/news/articles/2019-09-11/passive-u-s-equity-funds-eclipse-active-in-epic-industry-shift (accessed 30 March 2021)

14 P. Berger and T. Luckmann, *The Social Construction of Reality: A Treatise in the Sociology of Knowledge* (New York: Penguin Books, 1966).

15 Kay, *Other People's Money*.

16 J. Ryan-Collins, T. Greenham, R. Werner and A. Jackson, *Where Does Money Come From? A Guide to the UK Monetary and Banking System* (London, New Economics Foundation, 2011).

17 Kay, *Other People's Money*, 1.

18 R. D. Congleton, 'On the Political Economy of the Financial Crisis and Bailout of 2008–2009', *Public Choice* 140 (2018): 287–317.

19 E. Grossman and C. Woll, 'Saving the Banks: The Political Economy of Bailouts', *Comparative Political Studies* 47, no. 4 (2014), doi:10.1177/0010414013488540 (accessed 19 March 2021).

20 HMRC, *Corporation Tax (CT) statistics Commentary September 2020* (2020), HM Revenue and Customs, https://assets.publishing.service.gov.uk/government/uploads/system/uploads/attachment_data/file/919769/CT_stats_commentary_2020.pdf (accessed 30 March 2021). HMRC, *Corporation Tax Statistics 2018* (2018), https://assets.publishing.service.gov.uk/government/uploads/system/uploads/attachment_data/file/752467/181018_CT_stats_2018_-_11.1A_footnote_amendment.pdf (accessed 30 March 2021).

21 I have used corporation tax because the other tax revenues collected from the City, like income tax, could conceivably be covered by any other industry that would take up the

space finance is filling in our economy, if it were to vacate that space, and as such shouldn't factored into the City's self-justification rhetoric.

22 M. Keep, *Tax Statistics: An Overview* (15 February 2021), UK Parliament, House of Commons Library, https://commonslibrary.parliament.uk/research-briefings/cbp-8513/ (accessed 30 March 2021).

23 Kay, *Other People's Money*, 302.

24 CRESC, *An Alternative Report on Banking Reform* (Manchester: CRESC, 2009)

25 A. Baker, G. Epstein and J. Montecino, *The UK's Finance Curse? Costs and Processes* (Sheffield: Political Economy Research Institute, 2019).

26 Baker, Epstein and Montecino, *The UK's Finance Curse?*

Chapter 3 – Magic money tree: myth in the political sphere

1 D. Summers, 'Cameron Warns of New Age of Austerity' (24 April 2009) *The Guardian*, www.theguardian.com/politics/2009/apr/26/david-cameron-conservative-economic-policy1 (accessed 30 March 2021).

2 Business Innovation and Skills, but now, after a merger with the energy department, BIES.

3 S. H. Nothcote and C. E. Trevelyan, *Report on the Organisation of the Civil Service* [1713] (1854), Parliamentary Papers, XXVII.

4 Women were allowed to join in 1925.

5 Nothcote and Trevelyan, *Report on the Organisation of the Civil Service*, 111.

6 All interviewees in this chapter are quoted anonymously.

7 It is important to clarify that I focus here on the work conducted in government departments. Much government research is now tendered out to large insurance and financial corporations, but the discussion of these sites is beyond the scope of the chapter.

8 Cabinet Office, 'Civil Service Statistics', *Cabinet Office National Statistics* 31, no. 3 (2020), https://assets.publishing.service.gov.uk/government/uploads/system/uploads/

attachment_data/file/940284/Statistical_bulletin_Civil_Service_Statistics_2020_V2.pdf (accessed 30 March 2021).

9 Statistics attained through communication with the Government Economic Services and thanks to the courtesy of Professor Aeron Davis, along with this government blog: T. Bearpark, A. Heron and B. Glover, 'Economics in Government: More Open, More Diverse, More Influential', *Civil Service Quarterly* (8 August 2017), https://quarterly.blog.gov.uk/2017/08/08/economics-in-government-more-open-more-diverse-more-influential/ (accessed 30 March 2021).

10 See A. Davis and C. Walsh, 'The Role of the State in the Financialisation of the UK Economy', *Political Studies* 64, no. 3 (2015): 666–682; W. Hutton, *The State We're In* (London: Vintage, 1996); S. Strange, *States and Markets* (London: Continuum; 1988); K. Theakston, 'Whitehall and British Industrial Policy' in D. Coates and J. Hillard (eds) *UK Economic Decline: Key Texts* (London: Prentice Hall, 1995), 300–313.

11 E. Montuschi, 'Questions of Evidence in Evidence-Based Policy, *Axiomathes* 19, no. 4 (2009): 425–439.

12 The slightly less impressive name 'researcher' is used to denote other social scientists.

13 A. S. Hornby, *Oxford Advanced Learner's Dictionary of Current English*, ed. Jonathan Crowther (Oxford: Oxford University Press, 1995).

14 A quick google search for technician jobs confirms this.

15 For a discussion of natural metaphors and economic discourse see P. Mirowski (ed.) *Natural Images in Economic Thought: 'Markets Read in Tooth and Claw'* (Cambridge: Cambridge University Press, 1994).

16 Taking this base drive as a starting point is critical to a vision that prioritises a market economy, as it precludes the notion that anything other than a market society will be compatible with our fundamental nature as human beings. It also provides an objective premise from which economic knowledge can stem, allowing it to be presented as a rationalised discourse based on an identifiable objective fact (human beings are self-interested).

17 R. Partington, 'Rishi Sunak: Hard Choices Ahead to Tackle Debt from Covid Crisis', *The Guardian* (5 October 2020),

www.theguardian.com/business/2020/oct/05/rishi-sunak-debt-covid-crisis-tax-spending-cuts (accessed 30 March 2021).

18 'Rishi Sunak Gets 3 Things Wrong About Government Spending' (2 November 2020), YouTube video uploaded by Positive Money YouTube, www.youtube.com/watch?v=q1VU8Yjw-co&list=PLyl8oQTKiogMgciZPkXjp43eBh9uDsnh (0:15–0:40) (accessed 30 March 2021).

19 W. Brown, 'The Process of Fixing the British National Minimum Wage, 1997–2007', *British Journal of Industrial Relations*, 47 (2009): 429–443. doi:10.1111/j.1467-8543.2009.00722.x (accessed 11 March 2021).

20 Cameron claimed: 'Labour's plans for minimum wages, the Social Chapter and large increase in spending and taxes would send unemployment straight back up.' See the *Chronicle* (Stafford) (21 February 1996), referenced by M. Ion, 'Eroding Minimum Wages by Stealth', *The Guardian* (13 February 2009), www.theguardian.com/commentisfree/2009/feb/12/conservatives-minimum-wage (accessed 30 March 2021).

21 P. Cowley, 'When the Left Opposed a Minimum Wage' (31 August 2009), BBC News, http://news.bbc.co.uk/1/hi/uk_politics/8226421.stm (accessed 30 March 2021).

22 The nine LPC Commissioners had a secretariat of eight full-time civil servants who collated the evidence which the Commissioners based the rates on. The secretariat had a budget of £250,000 a year for research, which included commissioning reports from various organisations, frequently meeting with stakeholders (i.e. people who might be affected by changes in the NMW, businesses and employee groups) and condensing and feeding their results back to the Commissioners, who would then base the rate on negotiations around the evidence presented to them. Aside from the secretariat, there was also a team of nine civil servants who worked directly for the Minister in charge of the Department for Business Innovation and Skills. As well as presenting evidence to the LPC, this team sent out the remit to the LPC, and also fed back the LPC's report and recommendations to government ministers. The government then needed to accept the NMW rate before it was brought into effect; in the 16 years of the LPC's existence the government never once rejected the rate for the NMW that the LPC recommended.

23 O. M. Levin-Waldman, 'Why the Minimum Wage Orthodoxy Reigns', *Challenge* 58, no. 1 (2015): 29–50.

24 The headline-grabbing rate of £9.35 by 2020 is what they predicted 60% of the median hourly earnings for people over 25 would be by then.

25 *Tax Research UK* stated in a report that the 'Institute for Fiscal Studies is a body that persistently recommends tax increases that benefit the wealthiest in society at cost to those who make their living from work and the poorest in society.' Tax Research UK, *Is VAT Regressive and if so Why Does the IFS Deny it?* (2011), 13, www.taxresearch.org.uk/Documents/VATRegressive.pdf (accessed 30 March 2021).

26 Institute for Government, *The Cost of Coronavirus* (2021), www.instituteforgovernment.org.uk/explainers/cost-coronavirus (accessed 30 March 2021).

27 For a discussion of 'the lost decade' and the 'productivity problem' that includes the evidence I am calling on, see A. G. Haldane, 'The UK's Productivity Problem: Hub No Spokes', Academy of Social Sciences annual lecture 2018, www.bankofengland.co.uk/-/media/boe/files/speech/2018/the-uks-productivity-problem-hub-no-spokes-speech-by-andy-haldane (accessed 30 March 2021).

Chapter 4 – Media myths

1 E. Grieco, *US Newspapers Have Shed Half of Their Employees Since 2008* (Pew Research Center, 2020), www.pewresearch.org/fact-tank/2020/04/20/u-s-newsroom-employment-has-dropped-by-a-quarter-since-2008/ (accessed 30 March 2021). See also M. Barthel, *Newspapers: Fact sheet* (Pew Research Center: Journalism & Media, 2016), www.journalism.org/2016/06/15/newspapers-fact-sheet/ (accessed 30 March 2021).

2 D. Ponsford, 'Print ABCs: Seven UK National Newspapers Losing Print Sales at More Than 10% Year on Year' (2017), *Press Gazette*, www.pressgazette.co.uk/print-abcs-seven-uk-national-newspapers-losing-print-sales-at-more-than-10-per-cent-year-on-year/ (30 March 2021).

3 The small gains that have been made in online advertising have been offset by massive losses in print advertising. See A. Davis, *The Death of Public Knowledge: How Free Markets Destroy the General Intellect* (London: Goldsmiths Press, 2017).
4 The name of the publication and names of the people who work there have been changed to preserve anonymity. The magazine title has no affiliation with the organisation Money Matters.
5 For a discussion of how conceptions about the economy intertwine with wider views about society and human nature, see H. Miyazaki, 'The Temporalities of the Market', *American Anthropologist* 105, no. 2 (2003): 255–265. doi:10.1525/aa.2003.105.2.255 (accessed 29 April 2021).
6 The three companies are News UK, Daily Mail Group and Reach. Media Reform Coalition, *Who Owns the UK Media?* (2020), www.mediareform.org.uk/media-ownership/who-owns-the-uk-media (accessed 30 March 2021).
7 Kantola, 'On the Dark Side of Democracy'.
8 D. Tambini, 'What are Financial Journalists For?' *Journalism Studies*, 11, no. 2 (2010): 158–174.
9 Mike Berry's definitive 2019 book on the coverage of the financial crisis and the government's subsequent austerity programme deals with this theme at length. He shows how one simplistic but incorrect narrative came to dominate coverage, offering very little space for competing perspectives or discussion.
10 See: L. Bounegru and C. Forceville, 'Metaphors in Editorial Cartoons Representing the Global Financial Crisis', *Visual Communication* 10, no. 2 (2011): 209–229; Á Arrese and A. Vara-Miguel, 'A comparative study of metaphors in press reporting of the Euro crisis', *Discourse & Society* 27, no. 2 (2016): 133–155. doi:1177/0957926515611552 (accessed 29 April 2021); J. R. Horner, 'Clogged Systems And Toxic Assets: News Metaphors, Neo-Liberal Ideology, and the United States "Wall Street Bailout" of 2008', *Journal of Language and Politics* 10, no. 1 (2011): 29–49; W. Joris, L. d'Haenens and B. Van Gorp, 'The Euro Crisis in Metaphors and Frames: Focus on the Press in the Low Countries', *European Journal of Communication* 29, no. 5 (2014): 608–617. doi:10.1177/0267323114538852 (accessed 29 April 2021).

11 P. Berger and T. Luckmann, *The Social Construction of Reality: A Treatise in the Sociology of Knowledge* (New York: Penguin Books, 1966), 106.
12 Berger and Luckmann, *The Social Construction of Reality*, 107.
13 G. Lakoff and M. Johnson, *Metaphors We Live By* (Chicago: University of Chicago Press, 1980).
14 A. Smith, *Wealth of Nations* (1776), book 1, chapter 2, 26–27.
15 Kantola, 'On the Dark Side of Democracy', 211.
16 Lakoff and Johnson, *Metaphors We Live By*, 237.
17 J. Gittelsohn, 'End of Era: Passive Equity Funds Surpass Active in Epic Shift', Bloomberg (9 September 2019), www.bloomberg.com/news/articles/2019-09-11/passive-u-s-equity-funds-eclipse-active-in-epic-industry-shift (accessed 30 March 2021).
18 M. Coleman, 'SPIVA: 2020 Full-Year Active vs. Passive Scorecard', Index Fund Advisors (7 October 2020), www.ifa.com/articles/despite_brief_reprieve_2018_spiva_report_reveals_active_funds_fail_dent_indexing_lead_-_works/ (accessed 30 March 2021).

Chapter 5 – Demythologising the economy: not a pot of money

1 Positive Money/Dods, *Parliamentary Perceptions of the Banking System* (2014), http://positivemoney.org/wp-content/uploads/2014/08/Positive-Money-Dods-Monitoring-Poll-of-MPs.pdf (accessed 30 March 2021).
2 Positive Money, *How Much Money have Banks Created?*, https://positivemoney.org/how-money-works/how-much-money-have-banks-created/ (accessed 30 March 2021).
3 T. Piketty, *Capital in the Twenty-First Century* (Cambridge, MA: Belknap Press, 2014).
4 Kay, *Other People's Money*, 1.
5 See the Confederation of British Industries website on the financial services, www.cbi.org.uk/business-issues/financial-services/ (accessed 30 March 2021).

6 M. Wolf, 'The FED is Right to Turn on the Tap', *The Financial Times* (9 November 2009), www.ft.com/content/93c4e11e-ec39-11df-9e11-00144feab49a (accessed 29 March 2021).
7 G. Tullock, 'Paper money – A Cycle in Cathay', *The Economic History Review* 9, no. 3 (1957), doi.org/10.1111/j.1468-0289.1957.tb00671.x (accessed 29 April 2021); G. Davies, *A History of Money from Ancient Times to the Present Day* (Cardiff: University of Wales Press, 1994).
8 R. Werner, *New Paradigm in Macroeconomics: Solving the Riddle of Japanese Macroeconomic Performance* (London: Palgrave Macmillan, 2005), 167; Davies, *A History of Money*, 250.
9 Withers (1909), 20; quoted in Davies, *A History of Money*, 251.
10 For a fuller discussion see, among others: A. Jackson and B. Dyson, *Modernising Money: Why Our Monetary System is Broken and How it Can Be Fixed* (London: Positive Money, 2013); F. Coppola, *The Case for People's Quantitative Easing* (London: Polity Press, 2019); Ryan-Collins et al., *Where Does Money Come From?*; Werner, *New Paradigm in Macroeconomics*; A. Pettifor, *The Production of Money* (London: Verso, 2014); F. Doorman, *Our Money: Towards a New Monetary System* (North Carolina: Lulu, 2015).
11 Clark, 'What Were the British Earnings and Prices Then?'
12 UK house price index, *UK House Price Statistics* (2021), Land registry, https://landregistry.data.gov.uk/app/ukhpi/browse?from=1966-01-01&location=http%3A%2F%2Flandregistry.data.gov.uk%2Fid%2Fregion%2Funited-kingdom&to=2018-04-01&lang=en (accessed 31 March 2021).
13 Statista, *Median Annual Earnings for Full Time Employees in the UK from 1999 to 2020* (2020), www.statista.com/statistics/1002964/average-full-time-annual-earnings-in-the-uk/ (accessed 31 March 2021).
14 ONS, *UK House Price Index: March 2020* (2020), Office for National statistics, www.ons.gov.uk/economy/inflationandpriceindices/bulletins/housepriceindex/march2020 (accessed 31 March 2021).
15 Financial assets have now overtaken property in their ability to generate holding gains and, as such, also in their ability

to increase wealth inequality. A. Advani, G. Bangham and J. Leslie, *The UK's Wealth Distribution and Characteristics of High-Wealth Households*, The Resolution Foundation (December 2020), www.resolutionfoundation.org/app/uploads/2020/12/The-UKs-wealth-distribution.pdf (accessed 31 March 2021).

16 Kay, *Other People's Money*, 1.

17 Property being a prime example of a static asset that encourages speculation because – as we have seen – it generates holding gains.

18 Measures of wealth inequality suggest that it is twice as unequally held as income. See R. Crawford, D. Innes and C. O'Dea, 'Household Wealth in Great Britain: Distribution, Composition and Changes 2006–12', *Fiscal Studies* 37, no. 1 (2016). doi:10.1111/j.1475-5890.2016.12083 (accessed 29 April 2021).

19 Advani, Bangham and Leslie, *The UK's Wealth Distribution and Characteristics of High-Wealth Households.*

20 Christopher writes: 'Rentier capitalism is an economic system not just dominated by rents and rentiers but, in a much more profound sense, substantially scaffolded by and organised around the assets that generate those rents and sustain those rentiers.' B. Christopher, *Rentier Capitalism: Who Owns The Economy and Who Pays For it?* (London: Verso, 2019), xviii.

21 For other recent accounts of how this works see: A. Sayer, *Why We Can't Afford The Rich* (Bristol: The Policy Press, 2014); G. Standing, *The Corruption of Capitalism: Why Rentiers Thrive and Work Does Not Pay* (London: Biteback, 2016); M. Mazzucato, *The Value of Everything: Making and Taking in the Global Economy* (London: Allen Lane, 2018)

22 See Piketty's influential thesis that, left unrestrained, capitalism leads to a situation in which the level of return on capital outstrips economic growth, and, under these circumstances, societies become structured towards serving a minority of wealthy asset owners rather than the producers of goods and services. Piketty, *Capital in the Twenty-First Century.*

23 The Equality Trust, 'How Has Inequality Changed?' www.equalitytrust.org.uk/how-has-inequality-changed (accessed 31 March 2021).

24 For an extensive discussion of the 2007–2008 crisis, see A. Tooze, *Crashed: How a Decade of Financial Crises Changed the World* (New York: Viking, 2018).

25 The value of SPAC deals completed in 2019–2020 jumped 400%, and they raised $82.4 billion in IPO's (initial public offerings) compared to the $13.5 billion more traditional IPOs raised. See J. L. Rubinstien and D. Nussen, *Prime-time for SPACs* (8 March 2021), White & Case, www.whitecase.com/publications/insight/prime-time-spacs?utm_source=google&utm_medium=cpc&utm_campaign=Global_IPO&utm_content=Q12021GlobalIPO_SPACsGoogle&gclid=CjwKCAjwxuuCBhATEiwAIIIzoZ3K6WbeQVFJ41y7GTDFDw3iCJpxGhc92NVs-Xk42P5idJs304wcuRoCv1QQAvD_BwE (accessed 31 March 2021).

26 I have only sketched out some of the reasons why policy makers are unsuccessful in their current attempts to control the manner in which commercial banks create money. I would strongly encourage the reader to explore the arguments in more detail by reading other accounts, including: Werner, *New Paradigm in Macroeconomics*; Ryan-Collins et al., *Where Does Money Come From?*; Pettifor, *The Production of Money*; P. Mehrling, *The New Lombard Street: How the Fed Became the Dealer of Last Resort* (Princeton: Princeton University Press, 2011).

27 For a fuller discussion, see Ryan-Collins et al., *Where Does Money Come From?*, 64–71.

28 Ryan-Collins et al., *Where Does Money Come From?*, 103.

29 This also undermines capital adequacy ratios as a method for controlling bank credit creation. See Ryan-Collins et al., *Where Does Money Come From?*, 97.

30 K-S. Lee and R. Werner 'Reconsidering Monetary Policy: An Empirical Examination of the Relationship Between Interest Rates and Nominal GDP Growth in the U.S., U.K., Germany and Japan', *Ecological Economics* 146 (2018): 26–34.

31 Pettifor, *The Production of Money*.

32 Werner, *New Paradigm in Macroeconomics*.

33 For a detailed discussion of these ideas and other potential of ways of re-gaining the control of money supply see Ryan-Collins et al., *Where Does Money Come From?*, chapters 4–6.

34 Ryan-Collins et al., *Where Does Money Come From?*

35 For a history of the 100% reserves idea see: I. Fisher, '100 % money', *The Works of Irving Fisher*, Vol. 11, ed. W. J. Barber (London: Pickering & Chatto, 1997 [1935]); L. Currie, 'The 100 percent reserve plan', *Journal of Economic Studies* 31, no. 3/4 (2004) [1938], 355–365
36 Centre for Public Impact, 'Sparkassen Savings Banks In Germany', www.centreforpublicimpact.org/case-study/sparkassen-savings-banks-germany (accessed 5 May 2021).
37 D. De Burca, *The Role of Innovative Monetary Policies in Supporting a Green New Deal and more Sustainable Future for Europe and the World Resilience* (2015), 35, www.resilience.org/stories/2019-11-15/the-role-of-innovative-monetary-policies-in-supporting-a-green-new-deal-and-a-more-sustainable-future-for-europe-and-the-world/ (accessed 31 March 2021).
38 Ryan-Collins et al., *Where Does Money Come From?*, 47.
39 R. Werner, *Princes of the Yen: Japan's Central Bankers and the Transformation of the Economy* (New York: M. E. Sharp, 2003).
40 Werner, *New Paradigm in Macroeconomics*, 268.
41 There are a number of conditions that need to be met for a government to be in control of its own currency. Two key ones are that they can't hold significant debt in a foreign currency (this rules out many developing nations), or be part of a pan-national currency group that has sacrificed the power to create its own national currency (e.g. eurozone). As such, it is better to see the ability of states to determine the money supply as a spectrum, with the US at the top because the dollar is the global reserve currency, and then other countries, depending on their relative strength of their currency. Given that the pound is a well-established international currency the UK would be towards the top end of that spectrum and be able to exercise a good deal of control over the issuance of pounds. For an in-depth discussion see B. Bonizzi, A. Kaltenbrunner and J. Michell, 'Monetary Sovereignty is a Spectrum: Modern Monetary Theory and Developing Countries', in E. Fullbrook and J. Morgan (eds) *Modern Monetary Theory and its Critics* (Bristol: World Economics Association, 2019).
42 S. Kelton, *The Deficit Myth: Modern Monetary Theory and How to Build a Better Economy* (London: John Murray, 2020).

43 This is the point where mainstream economists demur, and talk of debt overhang.
44 For a fuller discussion of inflation and the capacity of the government to create a fairer and greener economy, see chapter 2 in Kelton, *The Deficit Myth*, or chapter 4 in Coppola, *The Case For People's Quantitative Easing*.
45 Fullbrook and Morgan, *Modern Monetary Theory and its Critics*; Kelton, *The Deficit Myth*; Ryan-Collins et al., *Where Does Money Come From?*
46 Bank of England, 'What is Quantitative Easing?' (5 November 2020), www.bankofengland.co.uk/monetary-policy/quantitative-easing (accessed 31 March 2021).
47 T. L. O'Brien and N. Kaissar, 'Covid Relief Bigger than World War II Budget? Sounds Right' (11 March 2021), Bloomburg, www.bloomberg.com/opinion/articles/2021-03-11/stimulus-checks-biden-s-war-on-covid-demands-wartime-spending?srnd=politics-vp (accessed 31 March 2021).
48 HMRC, 'HMRC Coronavirus (Covid-19) Statistics' (25 March 2021), www.gov.uk/government/collections/hmrc-coronavirus-covid-19-statistics (accessed 29 March 2021).
49 A small amount of QE (£20 billion) has been used to buy corporate bonds as well. Independent Evaluation Office, *IEO Evaluation of the Bank of England's Approach to Quantitative Easing* (2021), www.bankofengland.co.uk/independent-evaluation-office/ieo-report-january-2021/ieo-evaluation-of-the-bank-of-englands-approach-to-quantitative-easing#:~:text=As%20of%20November%202020%2C%20the,20%20billion%20of%20corporate%20bonds (accessed 31 March 2021).
50 Independent Evaluation Office, *IEO Evaluation of the Bank of England's Approach to Quantitative Easing*.
51 For accounts of the process behind financialisation, see: Kay, *Other People's Money*; G. Krippner, *Capitalizing on Crisis: The Political Origins of the Rise of Finance* (Cambridge, MA: Harvard University Press, 2011).
52 The Equality Trust, *The Scale of Economic Inequality in the UK*, www.equalitytrust.org.uk/scale-economic-inequality-uk (accessed 31 March 2021).
53 World Inequality Report (2018), https://wir2018.wid.world/part-4.html (accessed 31 March 2021).

54 It's hard to find precise figures for real wages as there are many factors at play but this ONS report from 2014 states that real wage growth has 'been on a broadly downwards trend' since the 1970s. C. Taylor, A. Jowett and M. Hardie, *An Examination of Falling Real Wages, 2010–2013* (2014), Office for National Statistics. This TUC report from 2019 shows this downwards trend continuing until more recent times: TUC, 'Labour Market Impact', in *Lessons From a Decade of Failed Austerity* (2019), www.tuc.org.uk/research-analysis/reports/lessons-decade-failed-austerity?page=2 (accessed 31 March 2021).

Index